Great Escapes
Europe

TASCHEN

Great Escapes
Europe

Texts by Shelley-Maree Cassidy   *Compiled and edited by* Angelika Taschen

Contents   Inhalt   Sommaire

Price categories:		Preiskategorien:		Catégories de prix :	
€	up to 150 €	€	bis 150 €	€	jusqu'à 150 €
€€	up to 250 €	€€	bis 250 €	€€	jusqu'à 250 €
€€€	up to 450 €	€€€	bis 450 €	€€€	jusqu'à 450 €
€€€€	over 450 €	€€€€	über 450 €	€€€€	plus de 450 €

On the Rocks...
Icehotel, Jukkasjärvi

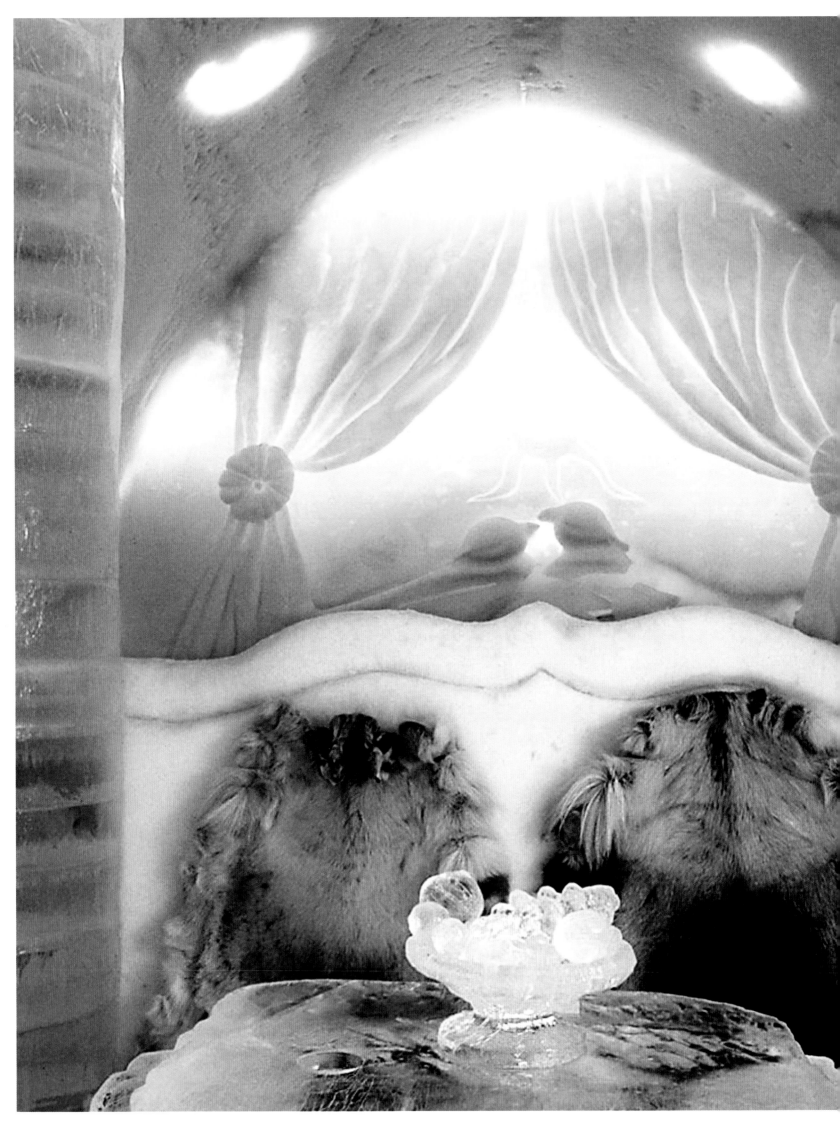

Icehotel, Jukkasjärvi

On the Rocks

This icy accommodation draws flocks of visitors each winter, deliberately seeking out its chilly walls and magnetized by the chance to spend the night in an igloo.

But this is, of course, not the usual sort of igloo. It is more of a frozen palace in the far north of Sweden. Within the sparkling blocks of ice, guests of the Icehotel will come to realize that "all that glitters is not gold". Rather, it is cold, very cold. And, in this case, this is a boon or else this impressive hotel would melt! Which it does, every year when spring arrives. Only to be sculpted again come winter. Ice provides the material for both the building blocks and the furnishings. Inside, it is 5–8 °C below zero (17.6–23 °F), which is quite mild when compared to the climate outside. The thick ice is almost soundproof, so even the noise of your teeth chattering will be muffled. But you'll be snug in an arctic sleeping bag on your ice bed draped with reindeer skins. A hot drink comes with the wake-up call, and a sauna will bring you back up to room temperature.

Another one of its attractions is the opportunity to see the stunning Northern Lights. Starry streaks of colour arch across the night sky in a painterly light show – another rare treat that nature has to offer during your frosty sojourn in Sweden's northern reaches.

**Books to pack: "Love in a Cold Climate" by Nancy Mitford
"Miss Smilla's Feeling for Snow" by Peter Høeg**

Icehotel	
981 91 Jukkasjärvi	
Sweden	
Tel: + 46 (0) 980 668 00	
Fax: + 46 (0) 980 668 90	
E-mail: info@icehotel.com	
Website: www.icehotel.com	

DIRECTIONS	200 km/124 m north of the Arctic Circle; 85-minute flight from Stockholm, 15 minutes from Kiruna
RATES	€€
ROOMS	60 rooms, including 20 ice suites; in the Icehotel 30 bungalows and 12 rooms
FOOD	The local inn serves delicacies with a Laplandic touch
HISTORY	The Icehotel opened its doors for the first time in 1990 and is built anew every winter
X-FACTOR	The chill factor and Northern Lights

Auf Eis gelegt

Das Leben in einem Iglu scheint eine magische Anziehungskraft zu besitzen, denn die Menschen strömen in Scharen an diesen eisigen Ort. Natürlich handelt es sich hier nicht um einen gewöhnlichen Iglu, vielmehr um einen zu Eis erstarrten Palast im höchsten Norden Schwedens. Das Icehotel ist der beste Beweis für das Sprichwort »Es ist nicht alles Gold, was glänzt«. Denn alles, was hier glänzt, ist eisig kalt, weil das Hotel sonst schmelzen würde. Und tatsächlich beginnt das Hotel, wenn der Sommer naht, zu tauen und verschwindet schließlich ganz. Jahr für Jahr wird es mitsamt der kompletten Einrichtung neu gemeißelt.

Die Temperatur im Inneren des Hotels beträgt -5 bis -8 C°, was verglichen mit der Außentemperatur geradezu mild erscheint. Die mächtigen Eisblöcke sind nahezu schalldicht, sodass nicht einmal das Klappern der Zähne zu hören ist. Doch auf dem mit Rentierfell bezogenen Eisbett, eingemummelt in den Polarschlafsack, ist es schön mollig warm. Mit dem morgendlichen Weckdienst wird ein heißes Getränk serviert, und ein Besuch in der Sauna bringt den Körper wieder auf Zimmertemperatur.

Eine weitere Attraktion ist die einmalige Gelegenheit, die grandiosen Nordlichter zu beobachten: jene in allen Farben erstrahlenden Lichtbögen am nächtlichen Himmel, die wie eine von Künstlern erschaffene Lightshow anmuten.

Buchtipps: »Liebe unter kaltem Himmel« von Nancy Mitford
»Fräulein Smillas Gespür für Schnee« von Peter Høeg

Avec glaçon

Un endroit glacial, mais on y va de son plein gré, tant est exaltante l'idée de séjourner dans un igloo.

Bien sûr, il ne s'agit pas de n'importe quel igloo. Parlons plutôt d'un palais gelé, tout au nord de la Suède. L'Icehotel est bien la preuve que «tout ce qui brille n'est pas or». Ici, tout ce qui brille est froid, glacé même, sinon l'hôtel fondrait. Ce qui se produit régulièrement. L'arrivée de l'été, en effet, le voit s'affaisser puis disparaître. Et chaque année, un nouvel édifice est sculpté dans la glace, murs et mobilier compris. À l'intérieur, il fait -5 à -8° C, ce qui n'est rien comparé à la température extérieure. Grâce à l'épaisseur de la glace, les chambres sont quasiment insonorisées, et c'est à peine si vous entendrez claquer vos dents tandis que vous vous loverez dans un sac de couchage polaire, sur un lit de glace recouvert de peaux de rennes. Une boisson chaude vous sera servie dès votre réveil, et un sauna vous remettra à température ambiante.

Parmi les autres attractions de l'hôtel figure la contemplation de l'aurore boréale : des arcs colorés illuminent la nuit comme dans un spectacle de lumières mis en scène par la Nature.

Livres à emporter : « L'Amour dans un climat froid » de Nancy Mitford
« Smilla et l'amour de la neige » de Peter Høeg

ANREISE	200 km vom nördlichen Polarkreis entfernt, ca. 85 Minuten Flug von Stockholm, von Kiruna 15 Minuten Fahrt
PREIS	€€
ZIMMER	60 Zimmer, inklusive 20 Ice-Suiten, im Icehotel 30 Bungalows und 12 Zimmer
KÜCHE	Das örtliche Gasthaus bietet Delikatessen mit leicht lappländischer Note
GESCHICHTE	Das Icehotel wurde 1990 eröffnet und wird jeden Winter neu aufgebaut
X-FAKTOR	Eisige Kälte und fantastische Nordlichter

ACCÈS	À 200 km au nord du cercle polaire arctique ; à 85 minutes d'avion de Stockholm, et à 15 minutes de Kiruna
PRIX	€€
CHAMBRES	60 chambres, dont 20 suites ; au Icehotel 30 bungalows et 12 chambres
RESTAURATION	L'auberge locale sert des spécialités lapones
HISTOIRE	Inauguré en 1990, l'Icehotel est a nouveau sculpté chaque hiver
LES « PLUS »	La glace, bien sûr, et l'aurore boréale

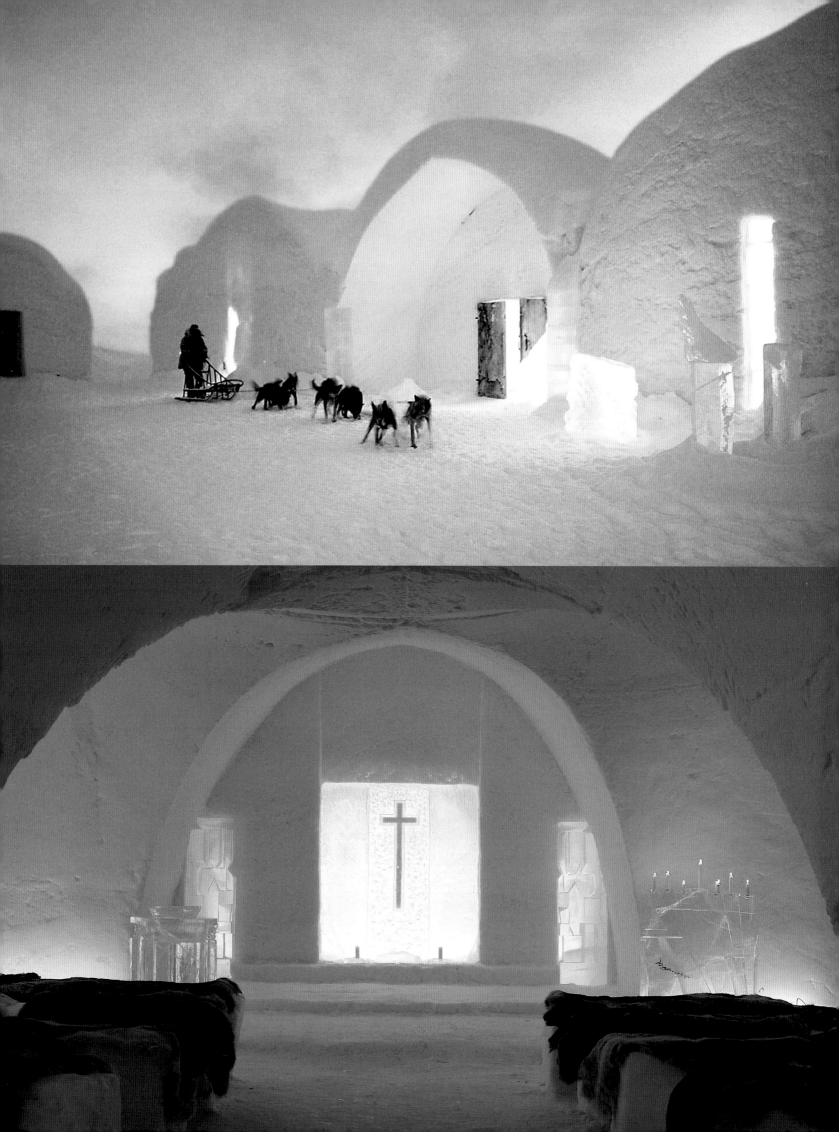

Norwegian Wood.
Røisheim Hotel, Lom

Røisheim Hotel, Lom

Norwegian Wood

Near the town of Lom in the "Land of the Midnight Sun" stands this quaint old farmhouse, boasting spectacular views of fjords far below. Reached via terrain that has been etched by ancient glaciers, beyond the country's highest mountain pass, this enduring abode has been here since the 17th century. Travellers of yesteryear who came this way have always stopped to rest here. And contemporary explorers can enjoy the same opportunity. Today, although at first sight it appears to still be an old farmhouse, it is a hotel.

Once you pass through the simple façade of this ancient building, you will find there is quite a plush interior. The charming style is one that respects its heritage, yet blends it with modern touches.

Røisheim Hotel is in the heart of one of the loveliest parts of Norway, most of which is a protected national park. You will see why the wild and beautiful region is called the "Home of the Giants" – two of the highest peaks in Europe give form to this impressive landscape. It is quite apt that a museum of mountains is to be found in Lom.

Book to pack: "Dreamers" by Knut Hamsun

Røisheim Hotel
Bøverdalen
2686 Lom
Norway
Tel: + 47 61 21 20 31
Fax: + 47 61 21 21 51
E-mail: post@roisheim.no
Website: www.roisheim.no

DIRECTIONS	350 km/220 m north-west of Oslo, 15 km/9 m from Lom
RATES	€
ROOMS	20 rooms in 13 cottages
FOOD	The food is a combination of traditional ingredients and modern cuisine
HISTORY	The oldest building was built about 1550, most of the others date from the 18th century. Røisheim has been receiving guests since 1858
X-FACTOR	Fantastic landscape with breathtaking views

Norwegisches Holz

Jenseits des höchsten Gebirgspasses im »Land der Mitternachtssonne«, eingebettet in eine von gewaltigen Gletschern geprägte Landschaft mit einem atemberaubenden Blick auf die Fjorde, befindet sich nahe der Stadt Lom dieses malerische alte Haus, in dem sich früher eine Poststation befand. Es wurde im 16. Jahrhundert erbaut und bot seit jeher Reisenden, die hier vorbeikamen, die Möglichkeit zu rasten, bevor sie ihren Weg fortsetzten. Zwar wirkt es auch heute noch auf den ersten Blick wie ein altes Bauernhaus, doch verbirgt sich hinter der einfachen Fassade ein äußerst elegantes Hotel. Die geschmackvolle Einrichtung legt Wert auf Tradition, ohne auf einen Hauch von Modernität zu verzichten.

Das Røisheim Hotel liegt in einer der herrlichsten Landschaften Norwegens, deren größter Teil Naturschutzgebiet ist. Sie werden es sicher schnell verstehen, warum man diese wilde, wunderschöne Gegend auch die »Heimat der Riesen« nennt. In dieser eindrucksvollen Landschaft befinden sich zwei der höchsten Berge Europas. Womöglich aus diesem Grund gibt es in Lom ein Bergmuseum.

Buchtipp: »Segen der Erde« von Knut Hamsun

Le bois norvégien

Au-delà du plus haut col montagneux du « Pays du soleil de minuit », près de la ville de Lom, sur une terre sculptée par les glaciers et entourée de vues spectaculaires sur les fjords en contrebas, se dresse une ferme datant du XVIe siècle. Autrefois, les voyageurs sillonnant la région y faisaient de courtes haltes avant de reprendre la route. Aujourd'hui, un hôtel est installé dans la ferme qui a conservé son aspect de jadis. La façade rustique cache un intérieur aussi confortable que douillet. Le charme de l'aménagement réside dans le respect du patrimoine mêlé à quelques touches modernes.

Le Røisheim Hotel se trouve en plein cœur de l'une des plus belles contrées de Norvège, dont la majeure partie est un parc national. Surnommée le « pays des géants », cette région compte deux des plus hauts sommets d'Europe. On ne s'étonnera pas qu'un musée de la montagne ait élu domicile à Lom.

Livre à emporter : « Rêveurs » de Knut Hamsun

ANREISE	350 km nordwestlich von Oslo, 15 km von Lom entfernt
PREIS	€
ZIMMER	24 Zimmer in 13 Häusern
KÜCHE	Eine Kombination aus einheimischen Zutaten und moderner Küche
GESCHICHTE	Das älteste Gebäude stammt von 1550, die meisten anderen wurden im 18. Jahrhundert erbaut. Seit 1858 empfängt Røisheim Gäste
X-FAKTOR	Herrliche Landschaft mit atemberaubenden Aussichten

ACCÈS	350 km au nord-ouest d'Oslo, 15 km de Lom
PRIX	€
CHAMBRES	24 chambres dans 13 maisons
RESTAURATION	Une combinaison d'ingrédients traditionnels et de cuisine moderne
HISTOIRE	Le bâtiment le plus vieux a été construit autour de 1550, la plupart des autres datent du XVIIIe siècle. Røisheim reçoit des hôtes depuis 1858
LES « PLUS »	Paysage merveilleux et vue à couper le souffle

A Castle of One's Own...

Amhuinnsuidhe Castle, Isle of Harris

Amhuinnsuidhe Castle,
Isle of Harris

A Castle of One's Own

A man's home is his castle, or so goes that old saw. Would that you could make this castle your home, at least for time, quite set apart from the rest of the world.

Amhuinnsuidhe Castle, on the Isle of Harris, is the most westerly castle in the whole United Kingdom. Built more than one hundred years ago, it stands at the edge of the sea in dramatic and beautiful surroundings. The castle's domain covers many thousands of acres, and is one of Europe's last unspoilt wildernesses. Although it is privately owned, it can be yours for a week. Set in a rugged landscape of mountains and glens, lochs and rivers, and white sandy beaches, it is world famous for its salmon and sea trout fishing. And it was here that the weaving of the classic Harris Tweed fabric first began.

This castle on the beach, sheltered at the head of its own bay, is also a citadel of cuisine. Fortunately, for a place so remote, this is a fortress that is full of great food. Amhuinnsuidhe is well known for its cookery school.

Rosemary, the castle's chef and host of a television cookery programme, makes full use of the rich local resources – lobsters and scallops fresh from the sea as well as venison and lamb.

Books to pack: "Mary Stuart" by Friedrich Schiller
"Ivanhoe" by Sir Walter Scott

Amhuinnsuidhe Castle

Isle of Harris

Hebrides PA85 3AS

Scotland

United Kingdom

Tel: + 44 (0) 1876 500 329

Fax: + 44 (0) 1876 560 428

E-mail: northuistestate@btinternet.com

Website: www.castlecook.com

DIRECTIONS	There is anchorage in front of the castle and a helicopter landing site. Stornaway airport on Isle of Harris, 1 hour by road, is 40 minutes flying time from Inverness, and 1 hour from Glasgow
RATES	€€
ROOMS	8 individually designed rooms
FOOD	Fresh seafood
HISTORY	Built for the Earl of Dunmore in 1867, now home of the Bulmer family
X-FACTOR	Romantic isolation and picturesque landscape

Ein Schloss für sich allein

»My home is my castle« lautet ein altes englisches Sprichwort. Dieser Traum von dem eigenen Schloss kann Wirklichkeit werden an einem Ort weit entfernt vom Rest der Welt. Das auf der malerischen Isle of Harris gelegene Amhuinnsuidhe Castle ist die am westlichsten gelegene Burg Großbritanniens. Sie wurde vor mehr als hundert Jahren direkt an der Küste inmitten einer aufregenden Landschaft erbaut. Über mehrere Tausend Hektar erstrecken sich die angrenzenden Ländereien, welche zu den letzten Flecken unberührter Natur in Europa gehören. Obwohl sich die Burg in Privatbesitz befindet, ist es möglich, sie für eine Woche sein Eigen zu nennen. Eingebettet in zerklüftete Berge und Täler, Seen und Flüsse sowie weiße Sandstrände, ist sie weltberühmt für den Fang von Lachs und Meeresforellen. Und hier war es auch, wo man anfing, den klassischen Harris Tweed zu weben.

Diese am Strand, im Schutz ihrer eigenen Bucht gelegene Burg ist zugleich ein Tempel der Kochkunst, der kulinarische Köstlichkeiten bereithält. Amhuinnsuidhe ist bekannt für seine Kochschule. Rosemary, im Fernsehen wie auch im wahren Leben die Küchenchefin, macht grosszügigen Gebrauch von dem, was die Natur hier in reichlichem Maße bietet: Hummer und Kammmuscheln frisch aus dem Meer sowie Wild und Lamm.

Buchtipps: »Maria Stuart« von Friedrich Schiller
»Ivanhoe« von Sir Walter Scott

Un château pour soi

«Mon chez-moi est mon château», dit un proverbe britannique. Qui n'a pas rêvé parfois de posséder sa propre forteresse et de vivre dans un château, loin du reste du monde... Amhuinnsuidhe Castle, sur l'île de Harris, est le château situé le plus à l'ouest de la Grande-Bretagne. Construit il y a plus d'un siècle, il se dresse au bord de la mer, à l'abri d'une baie privative, dans un environnement de toute beauté. Le domaine, qui couvre quelques milliers d'hectares, est l'un des derniers sanctuaires sauvages d'Europe. Bien que privée, cette demeure seigneuriale peut être la vôtre pendant une semaine. Nichée dans un rude paysage de montagnes, de glens, de lochs, de rivières et de plages de sable blanc, elle jouit d'une renommée internationale pour la pêche au saumon et à la truite de mer. C'est également ici que naquirent les célèbres filatures Harris Tweed.

Le château est en outre réputé pour sa gastronomie. Malgré son grand isolement, il offre une table délicieuse et est aussi très connu pour ses cours de cuisine. Rosemary, chef cuisinier à la télévision comme dans la vie, tire pleinement profit des nombreuses ressources locales – les homards, les coquilles Saint-Jacques, l'agneau et le gibier.

Livres à emporter : «Marie Stuart» de Friedrich Schiller
«Ivanhoé» de Sir Walter Scott

ANREISE	Die Burg verfügt über eigene Ankerplätze und einen Hubschrauberlandeplatz. Von Inverness bis Stornaway Airport auf der Isle of Harris 40 Minuten, von Glasgow eine Stunde Flugzeit; vom Stornaway Airport 1 Stunde Fahrt
PREIS	€€
ZIMMER	8 individuell gestaltete Zimmer
KÜCHE	Frischer Fisch und Muscheln
GESCHICHTE	Im Jahre 1867 für den Earl of Dunmore erbaut, heute im Besitz der Familie Bulmer
X-FAKTOR	Romantische Einsamkeit und malerische Landschaft

ACCÈS	Il existe un mouillage devant le château et un héliport. L'aéroport de Stornaway sur l'île de Harris est à une heure de route ; il relie Inverness en 40 minutes et Glasgow en 1 heure
PRIX	€€
CHAMBRES	8 chambres de style individuel
RESTAURATION	Poisson frais, moules
HISTOIRE	Construit en 1867 pour le duc de Dunmore, aujourd'hui en possession de la famille Bulmer
LES « PLUS »	Isolement romantique et paysage grandiose

The Luck of the Irish...
Belle Isle Estate, Fermanagh

Belle Isle Estate, Fermanagh

The Luck of the Irish

Whether you seek a cottage or a castle, like simplicity
or luxury, casting for fish or seeing the sights, the grounds of
this estate can offer you either, or both.

This is a somewhat different view of Northern Ireland, quite
unlike the one often shown in the past. There is no unrest
here; harmony, not friction, is to be found in this quiet cor-
ner of the Emerald Isle. The Belle Isle Estate is set apart
from the mainland; it is reached by a bridge that leads to this
hidden treasure. Spread over several islands on the lake of
Lough Erne, Belle Isle is true to its name. This peaceful
place is blessed with scenery to gladden the eye and the
heart, and its natural beauty ought to cheer up even the most
jaded.

A working farm on waters where the fishing is famed, Belle
Isle is one of the most historic sites in Ulster. It has been
inhabited since the 11th century, when the first voyagers
came to these shores. Bird life, too, has been shrewd enough
to throng here. For your sojourn in this serene setting, you
can nest in one of the charming cottages; stay in what was
once the coach house; or move into the grand old Mansion
House.

Book to pack: "Nora" by Brenda Maddox

Belle Isle Estate

Lisbellaw

Enniskillen

County Fermanagh BT94 5HG

Northern Ireland, United Kigdom

Tel: + 44 (0) 28 66387231

Fax: + 44 (0) 28 66387261

E-mail: info@belle-isle.com

Website: www.belle-isle.com

DIRECTIONS	115 km/71 m southwest of Belfast, 1.5 hours drive
RATES	€€
ROOMS	4 cottages, 2 apartments in the coach house, 8 courtyard apartments, and 9 rooms in the Hamilton Wing of the Mansion House
FOOD	Self-catering except for those staying in the Mansion House
HISTORY	Opened in 1992
X-FACTOR	Classic landscapes of Ireland at its greenest

Grüne Insel der Glückseligkeit

Egal ob Sie es schlicht oder luxuriös mögen, ob Sie lieber angeln gehen oder Sehenswürdigkeiten besichtigen – an diesem Ort können Sie sich für das eine oder das andere oder auch für beides entscheiden.

Nordirland präsentiert sich hier in einem ganz anderen Licht, als man es gewöhnt ist. Es gibt keine »Unruhen«, sondern nichts als Harmonie in diesem stillen Winkel. Die Belle Isle ist eine Inselgruppe im Lake of Lough Erne, die hält, was ihr Name verspricht. Vom Festland aus führt eine Brücke zu diesem gut verborgenen Juwel, dessen friedliche Atmosphäre und landschaftliche Schönheit das Auge erfreuen und das Herz erquicken. Und mag man noch so erschöpft sein, beim Anblick dieser überwältigenden Natur wird einem unwillkürlich leicht ums Herz.

Der Gutshof von Belle Isle, der für den Fischfang berühmt ist, gehört zu den ältesten Sehenswürdigkeiten von Ulster. Bereits im 11. Jahrhundert wurden die Inseln besiedelt und auch Vögel haben sich hier scharenweise einquartiert. Für Ihren Aufenthalt in diesem herrlichen Naturparadies können Sie entweder eines der zauberhaften Häuschen wählen, die einstige Remise oder aber das große alte Herrenhaus.

Buchtipp: »Nora« von Brenda Maddox

Bonheur irlandais

Que vous soyez amateur de cottage ou de château, que vous aimiez la simplicité ou le luxe, la pêche ou les excursions culturelles, vous trouverez l'un et l'autre dans ce merveilleux endroit.

C'est une facette de l'Irlande du Nord très éloignée de celle que l'on a l'habitude de voir. Point de « troubles » ni de violence ici ; une paisible harmonie règne dans ce petit coin de « l'île d'émeraude ». Le domaine de Belle Isle se trouve au large de la terre ferme : on rejoint ce trésor caché par un pont. Couvrant plusieurs îles du lac de Lough Erne, au cœur d'un environnement enchanteur, Belle Isle mérite bien son nom tant il est vrai que sa beauté naturelle réjouira les plus blasés d'entre vous.

Exploitation agricole prospère, au bord d'une eau poissonneuse, Belle Isle est l'un des plus anciens sites de l'Ulster. Il est habité depuis le XIe siècle, époque à laquelle ses rives furent découvertes. Une multitude d'oiseaux y a également élu domicile. Pour séjourner dans ce cadre paisible, vous avez le choix entre de charmants cottages, l'ancienne remise de voitures à cheval ou l'imposant manoir.

Livre à emporter : « Nora » de Brenda Maddox

ANREISE	115 km bzw. 1,5 Autostunden südwestlich von Belfast
PREIS	€€
ZIMMER	4 Häuschen, 2 Apartments in der Remise, 8 Apartments und 9 Zimmer im Hamilton-Flügel des Herrenhauses
KÜCHE	Selbstverpflegung außer im Herrenhaus
GESCHICHTE	Geöffnet seit 1992
X-FAKTOR	Klassischgrüne Landschaft Irlands

ACCÈS	À 115 km sud-ouest de Belfast, soit 1 heure 30 de route
PRIX	€€
CHAMBRES	4 cottages, 2 studios dans la remise, 8 studios sur cour et 9 chambres dans l'aile Hamilton du manoir
RESTAURATION	Cuisine à faire soi-même excepté au manoir
HISTOIRE	Ouvert en 1992
LES « PLUS »	Paysages classiques de la verte Irlande

Bird's-Eye View...
Iskeroon, Kerry

Iskeroon, Kerry

Bird's-Eye View

There are few places with a view that can match this one. The beguiling outlook is to be had from Iskeroon, one of the most secluded places to stay in Ireland. The house boasts a spectacular view of Derrynane Harbour, and out in the distance Deenish and Scarriff Islands. You can take a boat from the harbour to visit the Skellig Islands, once the site of a medieval monastic settlement – now it is home to huge colonies of nesting seabirds. For those seeking to settle for a time somewhere more comfortable than a rock ledge, Iskeroon is ideal. Any ruffled feathers will soon to be smoothed down by a few days in this peaceful guesthouse, itself a design jewel in a truly glorious setting. Iskeroon lies in the middle of a lush subtropical garden, laid out in the 1930s.

It includes many quite remarkable plants, like tree ferns and the very rare Kerry Lily. The path goes down to a private jetty and guests are welcome to go with the owners as they check their shrimp and lobster pots. Nearby is Caherdaniel, a quiet yet colourful village. Most importantly, it has a couple of pubs and a good restaurant. Aside from the scenery – which makes walking an obvious choice – there are opportunities to explore the surrounding hills and beaches on horseback.

Book to pack: "Angela's Ashes: A Memoir of a Childhood" by Frank McCourt

Iskeroon

Geraldine and David Hare
Caherdaniel
County Kerry
Ireland
Tel: + 353 (0) 66 9475119
E-mail: res@iskeroon.com
Website: www.iskeroon.com

DIRECTIONS	1.5 hours from Cork in the south-west of Ireland, and 4 km/2.4 m from the Ring of Kerry
RATES	€
ROOMS	3 rooms, 1 apartment
FOOD	Good choice of food at nearby pubs and Derrynane House
HISTORY	Built in 1936, Iskeroon was transformed 1995/96 and opened 1997
X-FACTOR	Bird's-eye view of the best scenery in southwest Ireland

Aus der Vogelperspektive

Es gibt nur wenige Orte mit einem Ausblick, der alles andere verblassen lässt.

Solch ein Panorama können Sie vom Iskeroon aus bewundern, einem der entlegensten Plätze Irlands. Vom Hotel aus haben Sie einen einmaligen Blick auf den Hafen von Derrynane und die nah der Küste gelegenen Inseln Deenish und Scarriff. Mit dem Boot erreichen Sie ebenfalls die etwas weiter entfernten Skelling Inseln, die einst Sitz eines mittelalterlichen Mönchsordens waren; heute nisten hier große Kolonien von Meeresvögeln. Wer sich aber gerne an einem bequemeren Ort als einem Felsvorsprung ausruhen möchte, für den ist das Iskeroon ideal. Schon nach wenigen Tagen in diesem in eine herrliche Landschaft eingebetteten architektonischen Kleinod hat man den Alltagsstress weit hinter sich gelassen. Iskeroon befindet sich inmitten eines üppigen subtropischen Gartens, der in den 1930er-Jahren angelegt wurde und in dem viele seltene Pflanzen wie Baumfarne und die Kerry-Lilie zu bestaunen sind. Ein schmaler Weg führt hinunter zur privaten Mole, wo die Hotelgäste den Eigentümern beim Prüfen der Hummer- und Garnelenkörbe zuschauen dürfen. Ganz in der Nähe liegt das ruhige, aber farbenprächtige Dorf Caherdaniel, das über einige Pubs und ein gutes Restaurant verfügt. Die Landschaft lädt zu ausgedehnten Wanderungen ein, aber es besteht auch die Möglichkeit, die angrenzenden Hügel und Strände auf dem Rücken eines Pferdes zu erkunden.

Buchtipp: »Die Asche meiner Mutter. Irische Erinnerungen« von Frank McCourt

À perte de vue

Il existe bien peu d'endroits au monde offrant un panorama d'une beauté aussi époustouflante.

Ce panorama, vous le trouverez à l'Iskeroon, l'un des endroits les plus reculés d'Irlande. Depuis l'hôtel, on a une vue spectaculaire sur le port de Derrynane et sur les îles Deenisch et Scarriff, proches du rivage. On peut aussi atteindre par bateau les îles Skelling, situées un peu plus au large, qui jadis abritaient un monastère médiéval et sont aujourd'hui peuplées d'immenses colonies d'oiseaux marins. Pour ceux qui rêvent de passer un séjour plus agréable que sur la crête d'une corniche rocheuse, l'Iskeroon est l'endroit idéal. Cette paisible pension de famille est un véritable petit bijou d'architecture, serti dans un somptueux écrin : un luxuriant jardin subtropical dessiné dans les années 1930. On y trouve des plantes remarquables, telles les fougères arborescentes et le rarissime simethis à feuilles plates. Le chemin descend jusqu'à une jetée privée, où les propriétaires possèdent des casiers à crevettes et à homards. Caherdaniel, un joli petit village réputé pour ses pubs et son bon restaurant, se trouve à proximité. Hormis les randonnées à pied, l'équitation est un autre moyen d'explorer les collines et plages environnantes.

Livre à emporter : « Les Cendres d'Angela : une enfance irlandaise » de Frank McCourt

ANREISE	1, 5 Stunden von Cork im Südwesten Irlands und 4 km vom Ring of Kerry entfernt
PREIS	€
ZIMMER	3 Zimmer, 1 Apartment
KÜCHE	Verpfelegungsmöglichkeiten in den nahegelegenen Pubs und im Derrynane House
GESCHICHTE	1936 erbaut, 1995/96 umgebaut und 1997 eröffnet
X-FAKTOR	Atemberaubender Ausblick auf die schönste Landschaft im Südwesten Irlands

ACCÈS	À 1 heure 30 de Cork au sud-ouest de l'Irlande, et à 4 km du Ring of Kerry
PRIX	€
CHAMBRES	3 chambres et 1 studio
RESTAURATION	Grand choix de restauration dans les pubs avoisinants et à la Derrynane House
HISTOIRE	Construit en 1936, transformé en 1995/96 et ouvert en 1997
LES « PLUS »	Vue panoramique sur le plus beau paysage du sud-ouest de l'Irlande

A Welsh Panorama...
The Lighthouse, Llandudno

The Lighthouse, Llandudno

A Welsh Panorama

Since 1862, the Lighthouse has watched over the waves that roll in and crash against the rocky limestone headland it stands on. Now the Lighthouse keeps guests, not sailors, safe from the elements, as an out-of-the-ordinary hotel. With its fortress-like appearance, the Lighthouse does not conform to the usual tower construction of most lighthouses. However, you will see that you are very high above the water when you look out of the dining room's tall windows and straight down at the dizzying drop some 100 metres (360 feet) to the sea below. The three suites all have spectacular views, from the Isle of Man to the north, to Puffin Island in the south. The lighthouse beacon was removed some years ago, and the glass panelled lamp room it once occupied is now a stunning sitting room, with a panoramic sea view through some 200 degrees east to west.

If you grow tired of looking out for ships on the horizon, you can walk in the nearby country park or visit the seaside resort of Llandudno, where Lewis Carroll wrote parts of his fabulous "Alice in Wonderland". Be sure to be back in time to watch the sunset from this most distinctive vantage point.

Books to pack: "To the Lighthouse" by Virginia Woolf "Alice in Wonderland" by Lewis Carroll

The Lighthouse
Marine Drive
Great Ormes Head
Llandudno
North Wales LL30 2XD
United Kingdom
Tel: + 44 (0) 1492 876819
Fax: + 44 (0) 1492 876668
E-mail: enquiries@lighthouse-llandudno.co.uk
Website: www.lighthouse-llandudno.co.uk

DIRECTIONS	1.5 hours' drive west from Manchester International Airport, 5 km/3 m from Llandudno railway station on the northern coast of Wales
RATES	€
ROOMS	3 rooms
FOOD	Fish restaurants in Llandudno
HISTORY	Built in 1862, the Lighthouse opened for the public in 1988
X-FACTOR	Keeping watch in your own tower

Von hoher Warte

Seit 1862 wacht der Leuchtturm nun schon über die Wellen, die ans Ufer rollen und sich an den Kalksteinklippen der Landzunge brechen, auf der er steht. Heute nimmt der Leuchtturm keine in Seenot geratenen Matrosen mehr auf, sondern beherbergt ein Hotel der ganz besonderen Art. Von außen wirkt The Lighthouse eher wie eine Festung als wie ein gewöhnlicher Leuchtturm. Wenn man aber hoch oben aus den schmalen Fenstern des Speisesaals hinunter in die Tiefe schaut, wird man sich seiner Schwindel erregenden Höhe von 100 Metern bewusst. Von jeder der drei Suiten aus hat man einen schönen Ausblick: nach Norden hin auf die Isle of Man, nach Süden auf Puffin Island. Das Leuchtfeuer auf der Spitze wurde vor einigen Jahren entfernt und das gläserne Laternendeck zu einem Aufenthaltsraum umfunktioniert, der einen Panoramablick von 200 Grad von Ost nach West ermöglicht. Wenn Sie es aber müde werden, Schiffe am Horizont zu beobachten, können Sie im nahe gelegenen Park spazieren gehen und das Seebad Llandudno besuchen, wo Lewis Carroll einen Teil seines wundervollen Romans »Alice im Wunderland« schrieb. Kommen Sie aber unbedingt rechtzeitig zurück, damit Sie nicht den Sonnenuntergang von diesem einzigartigen Aussichtspunkt verpassen.

Buchtipps: »Die Fahrt zum Leuchtturm« von Virginia Woolf »Alice im Wunderland« von Lewis Carroll

Une vue imprenable

Depuis 1862, le Lighthouse surveille les eaux impétueuses qui déferlent sur le promontoire de calcaire sur lequel il se dresse. Aujourd'hui, le phare transformé en un insolite hôtel accueille ses hôtes, bien à l'abri des éléments.
Ayant l'aspect d'une forteresse, le Lighthouse n'est guère conforme à l'idée que l'on se fait habituellement d'un phare. Toutefois, vous serez peut-être pris de vertige en regardant la mer, cent mètres plus bas, par les hautes fenêtres de la salle à manger. Les trois suites bénéficient toutes d'une vue spectaculaire, de l'île de Man au Nord à l'île Puffin au Sud. Le fanal du phare a été retiré il y a quelques années ; la salle vitrée qu'il occupait est devenue un magnifique salon d'où l'on jouit d'une vue panoramique de 200° d'Est en Ouest. Si vous vous lassez de contempler les bateaux qui passent à l'horizon, vous pouvez aller vous promener dans le parc proche ou visiter la petite station balnéaire de Llandudno où Lewis Carroll écrivit une partie de son magnifique roman « Alice au pays des merveilles ». Mais veillez à rentrer à temps pour admirer le coucher du soleil depuis ce point de vue privilégié.

Livres à emporter : «La Promenade au phare» de Virginia Woolf «Alice au pays des merveilles» de Lewis Carroll

ANREISE	1,5 Autostunden westlich von Manchester Airport, 5 km vom Bahnhof in Llandudno an der walisischen Nordküste entfernt
PREIS	€
ZIMMER	3 Zimmer
KÜCHE	Pubs und Restaurants in Llandudno
GESCHICHTE	Erbaut 1862, als Hotel 1988 eröffnet
X-FAKTOR	Wache halten im eigenen Turm

ACCÈS	À 1 heure 30 de route à l'ouest de l'aéroport de Manchester, et 5 km de la gare de Llandudno à la côte septentrionale du pays de Galles
PRIX	€
CHAMBRES	3 chambres
RESTAURATION	Pubs et restaurants à Llandudno
HISTOIRE	Construit en 1862, le Lighthouse est ouvert au public depuis 1988
LES « PLUS »	Monter la garde en haut d'un phare

GREAT ORME
LIGHTHOUSE
WARNING /
MERCHANT SHIPPING ACT 1894
57 58 VICT·CH·60·SEC·666·
ANY PERSON WILFULLY OR NEGLIGENTLY
DAMAGING THESE WALLS IS LIABLE TO
PROSECUTION TO A FINE NOT EXCEEDING
FIFTY POUNDS IN ADDITION TO THE COST
OF MAKING GOOD SUCH DAMAGE
LONDON E.C.3   BY ORDER
                      L.N POTTER

All Aboard...
The Old Railway Station, West Sussex

The Old Railway Station, West Sussex

All Aboard

Trains never arrive or depart on time, or indeed at any time, at this station. You can stay at The Old Railway Station without worrying about timetables and schedules, cocooned in a motionless carriage overlooking the pretty garden.

Trains once went through here on their way to and from Midhurst and Pulborough and on to London. Now the only ones left are Alicant, Mimosa, Flora and Montana, four Pullman carriages dating from 1912, 1914 and two from 1923 that have been beautifully restored into eight spacious and elegant rooms, all with en-suite bathrooms. Bearing little resemblance to their previous life as dining and parlour cars, the carriages, with their luxurious beds, plush furnishings, and soft colours, are a clever conversion of old to new. Appropriately, they are located next to the historic Victorian railway station, originally built in 1892 for the Prince of Wales, later Edward VII. Guests can choose to stay in the carriages or in either of two bedrooms in an annex to the station, whose former waiting room is now a splendid lounge for guests.

There is no waiting on a draughty platform or missed connections here, just old-fashioned peace and quiet. A treasure trove of antiques is in the local village.

Book to pack: "Stamboul Train" by Graham Greene

The Old Railway Station
Petworth
West Sussex GU28 0JF
United Kingdom
Tel: + 44 (0) 1798 342 346
Fax: + 44 (0) 1798 343 066
E-mail: info@old-station.co.uk
Website: www.old-station.co.uk

DIRECTIONS	84 km/52 m south of London, 30 minutes drive north of Chichester
RATES	€€
ROOMS	4 rooms on board, 2 in the station
FOOD	A 5-minute walk to award-winning local pub, the *Badgers Inn*, for lunch and dinner
HISTORY	The railway station was built in 1892
X-FACTOR	Living in a grown-up's train set

Alle an Bord?

An diesem alten Bahnhof kommen die Züge weder pünktlich
an noch fahren sie pünktlich ab, denn hier fährt überhaupt
kein Zug mehr. Sorgen Sie sich also nicht um Fahrpläne und
Abfahrtszeiten, sondern genießen Sie unbeschwert Ihren
Aufenthalt in The Old Railway Station, in einem der still-
gelegten Eisenbahn-Waggons mit Blick auf den bezaubernden
Garten. Denn von den Zügen, die hier früher auf dem Weg
nach London und Brighton hielten, haben zwei Wurzeln
geschlagen: Alicante und Mimosa, zwei Pullman-Wagen aus
der Zeit vor dem Ersten Weltkrieg, die liebevoll restauriert
wurden und jetzt vier geräumige und elegante Zimmer beher-
bergen, von denen jedes mit einem Bad ausgestattet ist. Ihre
Vergangenheit als Speisewagen sieht man diesen stilvoll
eingerichteten Waggons mit ihren luxuriösen Betten und
geschmackvoll abgestimmten Farben nicht mehr an. Sinniger-
weise wurden sie direkt neben dem historischen viktoriani-
schen Bahnhof platziert, wo die Gäste wahlweise auch in
einem der zwei Zimmer im Anbau des Bahnhofs Quartier
nehmen können, dessen Wartesaal zu einem romantischen
Empfangsraum umgebaut wurde. Vergessen Sie lange Warte-
zeiten auf zugigen Bahnsteigen und verpasste Anschlusszüge.
Hier finden Sie Ruhe und Frieden in nostalgischem Ambiente.
Das Örtchen Petworth ist eine Fundgrube für Antiquitäten-
liebhaber.

Buchtipp: »Orient-Express« von Graham Greene

Fermez les portières

Dans cette ancienne gare, les trains n'arrivent ni ne partent
jamais à l'heure : en fait, l'heure n'existe plus. À l'hôtel The
Old Railway Station, vous séjournerez confortablement dans
un wagon désormais immobile, avec vue sur un ravissant
jardin, sans avoir à vous soucier d'horaires ou d'agendas.
Les trains reliant Londres à Brighton passaient ici autrefois.
Aujourd'hui, il n'en reste plus que deux wagons, Alicante
et Mimosa. Ces voitures pullmans d'avant la Première Guerre
mondiale, magnifiquement restaurées, abritent désormais
quatre chambres spacieuses et élégantes, chacune équipée
d'une salle de bains. Judicieusement converties, avec leurs
lits luxueux, leur ameublement somptueux et leur décor
aux couleurs douces, elles ne gardent aucune trace de leur
ancienne fonction de wagon-restaurant. Elles sont stationnées,
comme il convient, à côté de la gare datant de l'époque victo-
rienne. On peut loger dans les voitures ou dans les chambres
aménagées dans une annexe de la gare dont l'ancienne salle
d'attente est aujourd'hui un splendide salon. Ici, tout est
calme et repos. Personne n'attend de train dans les courants
d'air d'un quai ou ne court pour éviter de manquer sa cor-
respondance. Au village, des trésors attendent les amateurs
d'antiquités.

Livre à emporter : « Orient-Express » de Graham Greene

ANREISE	84 km südlich von London, 30 Autominuten nördlich von Chichester
PREIS	€€
ZIMMER	4 Zimmer »an Bord«, 2 im Bahnhof
KÜCHE	In 5 Gehminuten erreichen Sie den preisgekrönten Pub The Badgers Inn (Mittag- und Abendessen)
GESCHICHTE	1892 wurde der Bahnhof erbaut
X-FAKTOR	Eisenbahn-Spielen für Erwachsene

ACCÈS	À 83 km au sud de Londres, à 30 minutes de route au nord de Chichester
PRIX	€€
CHAMBRES	4 chambres dans les voitures, 2 dans la gare
RESTAURATION	À 5 minutes à pied d'un pub primé, le Badgers Inn (repas de midi et du soir)
HISTOIRE	La gare existe depuis 1892
LES « PLUS »	Séjour dans un train nostalgique

Land Art Living...
Gunton Arms, Norwich

Gunton Arms, Norwich

Land Art Living

With the Gunton Arms, art dealer Ivor Braka has set the bar even higher: in 2009, together with his colleague Kit Martin, he bought up the ruins of an old guest house and carried out a detailed renovation programme. With only eight guest rooms, this boutique hotel now operates as a traditional pub. It speaks of British understatement, perhaps even British humour, because although the meat dishes in the Gunton Arms are cooked over an open fire, this technique now betokens real luxury – especially when your chef is Stuart Tattersall, previously responsible for the seafood at Mark Hix's in London's Mayfair. However, the most luxurious feature at the Gunton Arms is outside the front door: This boutique pub lies in the midst of a nature reserve of 400 hectares, where not only foxes and hares, but also owls and deer present their evening greetings from mist-enshrouded meadows. And there are 800 deer, by the way. All of this can be observed from the rooms with their traditional décor and every home comfort – from a velvet-upholstered armchair if you so desire. Or you can heave a sigh, put on your rubber boots and trudge through the dewy meadows as twilight falls. Not only wildlife and nature can be found in the floodplain of the parkland, but also sculptures by Sol LeWitt, Anthony Caro and Dan Graham (among others...). In the dining rooms of the Gunton Arms, also popular among residents of the picturesque environs, hang works by Damien Hirst and Tracey Emin. On a wall in the men's room there is even a work by Araki. Consummate understatement is still welcome in Great Britain: in 2013, the Gunton Arms was selected as Michelin Pub of the Year.
Book to pack: "Jane Eyre" by Charlotte Brontë

Gunton Arms
Cromer Rd, Thorpe Market
Norwich, Norfolk NR11 8TZ
United Kingdom
Tel: + 44 (0) 1263 83 20 10
E-mail: office@theguntonarms.co.uk
Website: www.theguntonarms.co.uk

DIRECTIONS	255 km north of London Heathrow, 25 minutes from Norwich Airport
RATES	€€
ROOMS	8 rooms, two living rooms (stamp rooms), which are intended only for hotel guests
FOOD	Regional and seasonal
HISTORY	The former gatehouse to a park that was created in the 18th century, and opened in 2011 for hotel and pub guests
X-FACTOR	English country life surrounded by contemporary art

Land Art Living

Mit dem Gunton Arms legt der Kunsthändler Ivor Braka die sogenannte Latte noch etwas höher: Gemeinsam mit seinem Kollegen Kit Martin erwarb er 2009 die Ruine eines alten Gasthauses und setzte ein detailverliebtes Sanierungskonzept um. Mit nur acht Gästezimmern firmiert das Boutique Hotel mittlerweile als Traditional Pub. Daraus spricht britisches Understatement, eventuell sogar britischer Humor, denn obwohl die Fleischgerichte im Gunton Arms auf einem offenen Feuer gegart werden, handelt es bei solcher Zubereitungstechnik mittlerweile um Luxus – vor allem wenn der Chefkoch Stuart Tattersall heißt und zuvor bei Mark Hix in London-Mayfair für die Fischspezialitäten zuständig war.

Der allergrößte Luxus des Gunton Arms ist aber vor der Tür des Hauses zu finden: Der Boutique Pub steht nämlich inmitten eines Naturschutzgebietes von 400 Hektar, wo sich auf nebelumflorten Wiesen nicht nur Fuchs und Hase, sondern auch Eulen, Rehe und Hirsche die Abendgrüße entbieten. Insgesamt 800 Hirsche und Rehe übrigens. All dies ist aus den traditionell mit allem Komfort eingerichteten Zimmern des Hauses zu beobachten, aus einer samtgepolsterten Ohrenchaise beispielsweise. Oder man legt seufzend die Gummistiefel an und stapft über die taufeuchten Wiesen gen Abendrot. Nicht nur Wild und Natur sind dort auf den Auen der Parklandschaft zu finden, sondern auch Skulpturen von Sol LeWitt, Anthony Caro und Dan Graham. Unter anderem. In den Speisezimmern des Gunton Arms, übrigens auch bei den Einwohnern des malerischen Umlandes beliebt, hängen Werke von Damien Hirst und Tracey Emin. Selbst an einer Wand in der Herrentoilette findet sich eine Arbeit von Araki. Gelungenes Understatement wird in Großbritannien nach wie vor gerne gesehen: Im Jahr 2013 wurde das Gunton Arms vom Guide Michelin zum Pub of the Year gewählt.

Buchtipp: »Jane Eyre« von Charlotte Brontë

L'art de vivre bucolique

Avec le Gunton Arms, le marchand d'art Ivor Braka place la barre supposée encore un peu plus haut : c'est en 2009 qu'il a acheté avec son collègue Kit Martin la ruine d'une ancienne auberge et s'y est livré à un programme de rénovation dans l'amour du moindre détail. Avec seulement huit chambres, le boutique hôtel se présente aujourd'hui comme un *Traditional Pub*. L'art britannique de l'euphémisme, voire l'humour british, y est cultivé car, si la viande du Gunton Arms est cuite directement au feu de bois, ce mode de préparation est devenu un luxe — surtout lorsque le chef porte le nom de Stuart Tattersall et a été auparavant responsable des spécialités de poisson chez Mark Hix, dans le quartier londonien de Mayfair.

Mais le plus grand luxe du Gunton Arms se trouve devant la porte : le boutique pub est situé au cœur d'un parc naturel de 400 hectares aux prairies voilées de brume où renards et lièvres, mais aussi hiboux, chevreuils et cerfs viennent le soir saluer les hôtes. Ils sont 800 cerfs et chevreuils. Le tout à observer depuis les chambres traditionnelles aménagées avec tout le confort de la maison, par exemple dans un fauteuil à oreilles aux coussins de velours. On peut aussi mettre en soupirant ses bottes en caoutchouc et marcher à travers prés dans l'herbe humide de rosée au coucher du soleil. Le gibier et la nature ne seront pas les seules rencontres dans les prairies du parc à l'anglaise, on y trouve aussi des sculptures de Sol LeWitt, Anthony Caro et Dan Graham. Et d'autres encore. Dans les salles à manger du Gunton Arms, également appréciées des habitants de cette campagne pittoresque, sont accrochées des œuvres de Damien Hirst et Tracey Emin. Et même au mur des toilettes pour hommes, on trouve un Araki. Aujourd'hui comme hier, l'euphémisme réussi est bien vu en Grande-Bretagne et, en 2013, le Gunton Arms a été nommé Pub of the Year par le Guide Michelin.

Livre à emporter : « Jane Eyre » de Charlotte Brontë

ANREISE	255 km nördlich von London-Heathrow, 25 min von Norwich Airport	ACCÈS	À 255 km au nord de l'aéroport London Heathrow, à 25 mn de l'aéroport de Norwich
PREIS	€€	PRIX	€€
ZIMMER	8 Zimmer, zwei Wohnzimmer (stamp rooms), die nur für Hotelgäste bestimmt sind	CHAMBRES	8 chambres, deux salons (stamp rooms) réservés aux clients de l'hôtel
KÜCHE	regional und saisonal	RESTAURATION	Cuisine régionale de saison
GESCHICHTE	Das ehemalige Pförtnerhaus zu einer Parklandschaft, die im 18. Jahrhundert angelegt wurde, eröffnete 2011 für Hotel- und Pubgäste	HISTOIRE	Ancienne loge du concierge d'un parc paysager aménagé au XVIIIe siècle, l'hôtel et pub a ouvert en 2011.
X-FAKTOR	englisches Landleben, umgeben von zeitgenössischer Kunst	LES « PLUS »	La vie champêtre à l'anglaise, au milieu de l'art contemporain

A Room with a View...
Maison Rika, Amsterdam

Maison Rika, Amsterdam

A Room with a View

Maison Rika belongs to the Swedish fashion designer Ulrike Lundgren, who is yet to become well-known outside her adopted country of the Netherlands. Located in the best area of the old city of Amsterdam, the De Negen Straatjes (Nine Streets), crisscrossed by canals, the narrow town house offers all the comforts that the world traveller on a shopping spree could wish for: tastefully furnished rooms with black painted floors and views over the Herengracht, adorned with works of art by Amsterdam local hero Sang Ming; black tiled bathrooms, copper washbasins and free WiFi on all floors. On the ground floor is the lobby, actually a shop, where alongside pieces from the collection of Ulrike Lundgren you can buy beautiful selected accessories, books, stationery, candles and jewelry. The upper two floors are devoted to the two hotel rooms, with double beds.

The Maison Rika has no restaurant, room service or breakfast, but along the canals, dozens of cafes, bars and restaurants can be found in easy reach.

Book to pack: "A Widow for One Year" by John Irving

Maison Rika
Oude Spiegelstraat 12
1016 BM Amsterdam
Nederland
Phone + 31 (0) 20330 1112
E-mail: rooms@maisonrika.com
Website: www.rikaint.com/sleep-under-the-stars

DIRECTIONS	In the heart of Amsterdam, a 5 minutes' walk from the main station, which can be reached in 15-20 minutes by train from Schipohl Airport
RATES	€€
ROOMS	2 rooms on the 2nd and 3rd floor, each occupying the entire floor
Food	There is no restaurant or breakfast. Many restaurants and small cafes such as Kaldi and To Go nearby
HISTORY	The building dates from the 19th century: it was used as a gallery and refurbished in 2012 by the designer Ulrika Lundgren, who opened it as a small concept store and "Hotel"
X-FACTOR	Impressive views of the historic Herengracht Canal and the brick façades

Zimmer mit Aussicht

Maison Rika gehört der schwedischen Modeschöpferin Ulrike Lundgren, die außerhalb ihrer niederländischen Wahlheimat noch zu entdecken ist. Im besten Viertel der Altstadt Amsterdams gelegen, dem von Kanälen durchzogenen De Negen Straatjes (Neun Straßen), bietet das schmale Stadthaus sämtlichen Komfort, den der weltweit Einkaufsbummelnde sucht: geschmackvoll eingerichtete Zimmer mit schwarz lackierten Fußböden und Ausblicken auf die Herengracht, die mit Kunstwerken des Amsterdamer Local Hero Sang Ming ausgestattet sind; schwarz gefliese Badezimmer, kupferne Waschbecken und kostenloses WiFi auf allen Etagen. Im Erdgeschoss befindet sich die Lobby, eigentlich ein Ladengeschäft, in dem neben Teilen aus der Kollektion von Ulrike Lundgren auch schöne ausgewählte Accessoires, Bücher, Schreibwaren, Kerzen und Schmuck verkauft werden. Die oberen beiden Etagen sind den insgesamt zwei Gästezimmern mit Doppelbetten vorbehalten.

Das Maison Rika bietet kein Restaurant, keinen Zimmerservice und auch kein Frühstück an, aber entlang der Grachten finden sich Dutzende Cafés, Bars und Restaurants im Pantoffelradius.

Buchtipp: »Witwe für ein Jahr« von John Irving

Chambre avec vue

La Maison Rika appartient à la créatrice de mode suédoise Ulrike Lundgren, dont la marque reste confidentielle hors des Pays-Bas, sa patrie d'adoption. Située dans le meilleur quartier de la vieille ville parcouru de canaux, De Negen Straatjes (Les Neuf Rues), l'étroite maison de ville offre tout le confort voulu aux amateurs de lèche-vitrines international : des chambres aménagées avec goût, au sol laqué de noir et vues sur le canal Herengracht, décorées d'œuvres du héros local amstellodamien Sang Ming ; des salles de bains carrelées de noir, des lavabos en cuivre et une connexion WiFi gratuite à tous les étages. Au rez-de-chaussée, le lobby est en fait une boutique avec, en plus d'objets de la collection d'Ulrike Lundgren, une sélection de beaux accessoires, livres, articles de papeterie, bougies et bijoux. Les deux étages supérieurs sont réservés aux deux chambres d'hôtes à lits doubles. La Maison Rika ne propose ni restaurant, ni service d'étage, ni petit déjeuner, mais on trouve des dizaines de cafés, bars et restaurants le long des Grachten, quasiment sans sortir de chez soi.

Livre à emporter : « Une veuve de papier » de John Irving

ANREISE	5 Gehminuten vom Hauptbahnhof, dorthin 15-20 Min mit dem Zug vom Flughafen Schiphol	ACCÈS	À 5 minutes à pied de la gare centrale, à 15-20 minutes en train de l'aéroport Schiphol
PREIS	€€	PRIX	€€
ZIMMER	2 Zimmer auf dem 2. und 3. Stockwerk, die jeweils die ganze Etage einnehmen	CHAMBRES	2 chambres aux 2e et 3e étages, qui occupent chacune tout l'étage
KÜCHE	Es gibt kein Restaurant oder Frühstück. Viele Restaurants und Cafés wie Kaldi und To Go sind 2–5 Min entfernt	RESTAURATION	Pas de restaurant ni de petit déjeuner. De nombreux restaurants et petits cafés, comme Kaldi et To Go, sont éloignés de 2 à 5 minutes
GESCHICHTE	Das Gebäude stammt aus dem 19. Jahrhundert, wurde als Galerie benutzt und 2012 von der Designerin Ulrika Lundgren eingerichtet und als kleiner Concept Store und „Hotel" eröffnet	HISTOIRE	Le bâtiment date du XIXe siècle, a été utilisé comme galerie, puis aménagé en 2012 par la designer Ulrika Lundgren qui y a ouvert un petit concept store et « hôtel »
X-FAKTOR	stimmungsvolle Ausblicke auf den historischen Herengracht Canal und die Backsteinfassaden	LES « PLUS »	Vues sentimentales sur le canal historique Herengracht et les façades de briques

Remembrance of Times Past

Seehotel am Neuklostersee, Mecklenburg

Seehotel am Neuklostersee, Mecklenburg

Remembrance of Times Past

This seems like a place that is kept in the memory, of a blissful childhood holiday; a summer spent by a lake. A place there used to be when one was very young and carefree. Long warm days in the sun and fresh air; untroubled by the stresses and strains that come with adulthood. This is evocative of that age, where "grown-ups" may recall some of the gentle times of their lost youth. The Seehotel is on the shores of Lake Neukloster; in surroundings so peaceful it is almost like being in a dream. The hotel's simple design is in accord with its country setting.

While its style appears to be classic, there is a modern overlay that makes it more chic than rustic. Being in this tranquil atmosphere, of white and cream, of natural colours and textures, gives a welcome soft focus on the world. In a boat on the lake, drifting through the reeds; cocooned in a wicker bathing chair reading, asleep, or just gazing at the sparkling water; there is no hurry here, no need to do anything taxing. Whether picking wildflowers, fishing from the end of the jetty, or merely daydreaming; staying here can all be part of going back, just for a short time, to a simpler way of life.

Books to pack: "Flights of Love" by Bernhard Schlink
"Elective Affinities" by Johann Wolfgang von Goethe

Seehotel am Neuklostersee	
Seestrasse 1	
23992 Nakenstorf bei Neukloster	
Germany	
Tel: + 49 (0) 38422 4570	
Fax: + 49 (0) 38422 45717	
E-mail: seehotel@nalbach-architekten.de	
Website: www.Seehotel-Neuklostersee.de	

DIRECTIONS	15 km/9 m east from Wismar, 2.5 hours' drive from either Berlin or Hamburg
RATES	€
ROOMS	11 rooms, 12 suites and 3 bungalows
FOOD	"AllesIsstGut" serves regional cuisine with select seasonal ingredients
HISTORY	The house was built at the beginning of the 19th century. During the GDR it served as a holiday resort. The hotel was opened in 1993
X-FACTOR	Back to the way things were …

Erinnerung an alte Zeiten

Der Ort wirkt wie ein Bild aus Kindertagen, als man unbe-
schwerte Sommerferien am See genoss. Dies scheint der Ort
zu sein, an dem man weilte, als man noch jung und frei von
Sorgen war und lange, warme Tage im Sonnenschein und an
der frischen Luft verbrachte ohne jeden Zwang und Druck.
Dieser zauberhafte Ort vermag es, Sie in die glückliche Zeit
Ihrer Jugend zurückzuversetzen. Am Ufer des Neukloster-
sees gelegen, ist das Seehotel eingebettet in eine friedliche
Landschaft, wie man sie sonst nur aus Träumen kennt.
Die schlichte Bauweise des Hotels steht in Einklang mit der
ländlichen Umgebung. Obwohl es auf den ersten Blick recht
traditionell erscheint, wirkt es nach steter Modernisierung
nicht rustikal: die neue »Badescheune« samt Schwimmbad,
das »Wohlfühlhaus«, die "Gänsebar" und das »Kinderhotel«
vervollständigen die Anlage und sind Orte, die entdeckt werden möchten. In einem Boot durch das Schilfrohr treiben,
in einem Strandkorb gemütlich lesen, schlafen oder einfach
nur auf das vor sich hin plätschernde Wasser blicken – es
besteht kein Grund zur Eile, es gibt nichts, was nicht auch
warten könnte. Egal ob man Wildblumen pflückt, am Ende
der Mole angelt oder einfach nur in den Tag hinein träumt –
hier an diesem Ort gelingt es einem, wenigstens für eine
kurze Zeit einen kleinen Schritt zurückzutun zu einem ein-
facheren und sorgloseren Leben.

Buchtipps: »Liebesfluchten« von Bernhard Schlink
»Die Wahlverwandtschaften« von Johann Wolfgang von Goethe

Souvenirs des temps passés

C'est un endroit qui évoque des souvenirs d'enfance, ceux
de merveilleuses vacances estivales passées au bord d'un lac.
Un de ces endroits que l'on associe à sa jeunesse insouciante,
à de longues journées chaudes remplies de soleil et de bon
air, exemptes des contraintes et des soucis qu'apporte la vie
adulte. Au Seehotel, les « grands » replongeront avec délices
dans les réminiscences de leur jeunesse perdue… Le complexe
s'étend sur les rives du lac Neukloster, dans un cadre si paisible que l'on se croirait dans un rêve.
L'architecture simple de l'hôtel est en parfaite symbiose avec
son environnement. En apparence de style traditionnel, l'établissement est doté d'un confort moderne qui le rend plus
chic que rustique. L'ambiance paisible, faite de blanc et crème,
de textures et couleurs naturelles, adoucit les âmes. Un tour
en bateau à travers les roseaux du lac, une sieste, une heure
de lecture ou de rêverie, installé dans un confortable fauteuil
en osier, au bord de l'eau… Ici, les journées se déroulent sans
hâte ni précipitation. Que l'on aille cueillir des fleurs sauvages,
pêcher au bout de la jetée ou que l'on se relaxe tout simplement, séjourner dans cet endroit fait retrouver un mode
de vie plus simple, près de la nature.

Livres à emporter : « Amours en fuite » de Bernhard Schlink
« Les Affinités électives » de Johann Wolfgang von Goethe

ANREISE	15 km von Wismar, 2,5 Autostunden nördlich von Berlin und östlich Hamburg	ACCÈS	À 15 km de Wismar et à 2 heures 30 de route au nord de Berlin et à l'est de Hambourg
PREIS	€	PRIX	€
ZIMMER	11 Zimmer, 12 Suiten, 3 Ferienhäuser	CHAMBRES	11 chambres, 12 suites, 3 bungalows
KÜCHE	»AllesIsstGut« bietet regionale Küche mit feinen saisonalen Zutaten	RESTAURATION	« AllesIsstGut » propose une cuisine régionale raffinée variant les ingrédients selon les saisons
GESCHICHTE	Das Steinhaus wurde Anfang des 20. Jahrhunderts gebaut und war zu DDR-Zeiten ein Ferienheim der LPG. Als Hotel öffnete die Anlage 1993. 2004 wurde sie um die »Badescheune«, 2010 um das »Kinderhotel« und 2011 um das »Wohlfühlhaus« erweitert	HISTOIRE	Construit à la fin du XXe siècle, le bâtiment était un centre de vacances sous la RDA. L'hôtel a ouvert ses portes en 1993. Il fut agrandi en 2004 avec la « Badescheune », en 2010 avec le « Kinderhotel » et en 2011 avec la « Wohlfühlhaus »
X-FAKTOR	Eine Reise zurück in die Vergangenheit	LES « PLUS »	Comme au bon vieux temps …

Perfect Peace and Deep Quiet

Landhaus Börmoos, Schleswig-Holstein

Landhaus Börmoos,
Schleswig-Holstein

Perfect Peace and Deep Quiet

They say that the air here is more sparkling than champagne; that the landscape is balm for the soul. High praise and claims indeed for the land of Schleswig-Holstein. This countryside between two seas, the Baltic and the North, is one of pleasing contrasts. Gentle hills, roads lined with trees, sleepy villages, fresh air, the sun reflecting on the waves; this is country life at its best. A trip to this part of the world will quite likely cause one to contemplate moving here. The owners of this lovely old farmhouse thought that too, when they saw this haven nestled in the landscape. So they did.

In the midst of fields and moorland, near lakes and very close to the coast, it is in an idyllic spot. Both Landhaus Börmoos and the barn have been restored to mint condition.

Under the thatched roof and beamed ceilings are charming rooms with huge alcove beds; once they have got used to the lack of noise these may be some of the best nights of sleep that guests experience. A weekend or longer here, with good food and wine, and pleasant strolls along the beach or by the lakes, would be bliss indeed. And for those who must hit a ball, there is a splendid golf course nearby.

Book to pack: "Effie Briest" by Theodor Fontane

Landhaus Börmoos	
Grüfft 9	
24972 Steinbergkirche/Habernis	
Germany	
Tel: + 49 (0) 4632 7621	
Fax: + 47 (0) 4632 1429	
E-mail: landhaus.boermoos@t-online.de	
Website: www.landhaus-boermoos.de	

DIRECTIONS	About 180 km north of Hamburg, nearest town is Flensburg, very near the Danish border
RATES	€
ROOMS	8 apartments for 2-5 guests respectively, in the main house/building and the adjoining barn, all equipped with a built-in kitchen
FOOD	Breakfast rolls can be delivered/available on request
HISTORY	The house and the barn were built in 1876 and the Landhaus Börmoos has received guests since 1985
X-FACTOR	The quiet that prevails

Tiefer Frieden und vollkommene Ruhe

Man sagt, die Luft hier sei besser als Champagner und die Landschaft Balsam für die Seele – ein hohes Lob für das Land Schleswig-Holstein. Die Region zwischen Ostsee und Nordsee ist reich an Kontrasten: Geschwungene Hügellandschaften, lange Alleen, verschlafene Dörfchen, viel frische Luft und die Sonne, die auf den Wellen der Meere glitzert – so lässt es sich auf dem Lande aushalten!

Eine Reise zu diesem Fleckchen Erde wird in jedem den Wunsch hervorrufen, hier zu wohnen. Nicht anders erging es den Besitzern dieses wunderschönen alten Bauernhauses, das sich harmonisch in die Landschaft einfügt, als sie es zum ersten Mal sahen. Und sie setzten ihren Wunsch in die Tat um. Inmitten von Feldern und Moorlandschaften, in der unmittelbaren Nähe von Seen und der Ostseeküste ist hier ein überaus idyllischer Ort entstanden. Das Haus und die ehemalige Scheune sind beide perfekt restauriert. Unter einem Reetdach und von massiven Holzbalken getragenen Decken befinden sich gemütliche Zimmer mit riesigen Alkovenbetten, in denen die Gäste den vielleicht besten Schlaf ihres Lebens genießen – wenn sie sich erst an die Stille gewöhnt haben. Ein Wochenende oder ein längerer Aufenthalt mit gutem Essen und gutem Wein, mit traumhaften Spaziergängen am Strand oder an den Seen ist wahre Glückseligkeit. Und wem das zu viel der Ruhe ist, der darf sich auf dem nahe gelegenen Golfplatz betätigen.

Buchtipp: »Effie Briest« von Theodor Fontane

Silence et sérénité

On dit qu'ici, l'air est plus pétillant que le champagne et que la nature apaise les âmes. Bref, on ne tarit pas d'éloges sur le Land de Schleswig-Holstein. S'étirant entre deux mers, la Baltique et la mer du Nord, la région offre de plaisants contrastes. Avec ses paysages vallonnés, ses routes bordées d'arbres, ses villages endormis, son air vif et piquant, son soleil se réfléchissant sur les vagues, elle incarne la douceur de la vie champêtre.

Il y a fort à parier qu'un séjour dans cette partie du monde vous donnera envie d'y rester pour toujours. En tous les cas, c'est l'idée qu'ont eue les propriétaires de Börmoos en découvrant cette ravissante ferme nichée dans la campagne. Ils s'y sont installés. Börmoos est un endroit tout simplement idyllique, situé au coeur de champs et de landes, non loin de jolis lacs et tout près du littoral. La ferme et la grange ont été entièrement remises à neuf. Le toit de chaume et les plafonds aux poutres apparentes abritent de charmantes chambres dotées d'immenses lits en alcôve. Une fois accoutumés à l'absence de tout bruit, les hôtes pourront goûter un sommeil comme ils en ont rarement connu. Un week-end ou quelques jours passés dans cette auberge, agrémentés d'une cuisine et de vins de qualité ainsi que d'agréables promenades au bord de la plage ou des lacs, vous laisseront un souvenir impérissable. Pour les inconditionnels, un superbe terrain de golf se trouve juste à côté.

Livre à emporter: «Effie Briest» de Theodor Fontane

ANREISE	Etwa 180 km nördlich von Hamburg und nahe der dänischen Grenze beim Städtchen Habernis gelegen
PREIS	€
ZIMMER	8 Apartments für je 2–5 Gäste im Haupthaus und anliegender Scheune, jeweils ausgestattet mit komplett eingerichteter Küche
KÜCHE	Auf Wunsch Brötchenservice
GESCHICHTE	Haupthaus und Scheune stammen aus dem Jahr 1876. Das Landhaus Bömoos empfängt seit 1985 Gäste
X-FAKTOR	Ruhe überall

ACCÈS	Environ 180 km au nord de Hambourg, tout près de la frontière danoise; la ville la plus proche est Habernis
PRIX	€
CHAMBRES	8 appartements pour 2 à 5 personnes, dans la ferme ou la grange adjacente, chacun équipé d'une cuisine complète
RESTAURATION	Service de petits pains à volonté
HISTOIRE	La ferme et la grange datent de 1876. L'hôtel a ouvert ses portes en 1985
LES «PLUS»	Calme et paix

Royal Antecedents...
Golfhotel Kaiserin Elisabeth, Bayern

Golfhotel Kaiserin Elisabeth, Bayern

Royal Antecedents

They will put up with imperious conduct here; but only if you can claim to be one of the crowned heads of Europe. There is a proud tradition of royalty in this place.

For 25 years, this is where the Empress of Austria chose to spend her summer holiday. The childhood home of Elisabeth, or Sissi, as she was lovingly called, was near here. After she was married, she often came back to see her family. She was the most famous guest of this 200-year-old inn and did not tire of coming here. And as a large entourage escorted her, she no doubt was the most valued of guests. After her life had been so cruelly put to an end in Geneva, the Hotel Kaiserin Elisabeth was named in her honour. A statue of her is to be found in the gardens. It is placed where she often sat, gazing across the lake towards the foothills of the Alps. The landscape is one of this place's most attractive features; another is the renowned golf course. Those who don't play can stay on the terrace, reading or writing poetry, just as the Empress once did. Going to see the castles built by her cousins, such as King Ludwig II, is one of many other options. **Book to pack: "Death by Fame: A Life of Elisabeth, Empress of Austria" by Andrew Sinclair**

Hotel Kaiserin Elisabeth
Tutzinger Straße 2-6
82340 Feldafing
Germany
Tel: + 49 (0) 8157 9309-0
Fax: + 49 (0) 8157 9309-133
E-mail: info@kaiserin-elisabeth.de
Website: www.kaiserin-elisabeth.de

DIRECTIONS	30 km/19 m south of Munich
RATES	€€
ROOMS	65 rooms
FOOD	German and Austrian specialities
HISTORY	Built in the 19th century, the hotel has been enlarged and renovated several times since then
X-FACTOR	The romantic view and history

Adel verpflichtet

Hoheitsvolles Gebaren würde man hier sicherlich dulden. Allerdings nur, wenn Sie beweisen können, eines der gekrönten Häupter Europas zu sein. Denn man ist stolz auf die eigene königliche Tradition.

25 Jahre lang verbrachte Ihre Kaiserliche Hoheit Elisabeth, Kaiserin von Österreich und Königin von Ungarn, hier ihren Sommerurlaub. Auch steht das Haus, in dem Sissi, wie sie meist genannt wurde, aufwuchs, nicht weit von hier; und nach ihrer Heirat kehrte sie oft hierher zurück, um die Familie zu besuchen.

Sissi war der berühmteste Gast in diesem 200 Jahre alten Gasthof. Und da sie mit großem Gefolge anzureisen pflegte, gehörte sie zweifelsohne auch zu den beliebtesten. Und Elisabeth schien dieses Orts nicht müde zu werden. Nach ihrem Tod durch ein Attentat nannte sich das Hotel ihr zu Ehren Hotel Kaiserin Elisabeth. Im Garten des Hotels wurde eine Statue von ihr genau an dem Platz aufgestellt, an dem sie oft saß, um den Blick über den See und auf die Ausläufer der Alpen zu genießen.

Neben der herrlichen Landschaft ist ein weiterer Anziehungspunkt der berühmte Golfplatz. Wer aber nicht Golf spielt, kann auf Elisabeths Spuren wandeln, auf der Terrasse ruhen, lesen oder Gedichte schreiben, genau wie sie damals. Natürlich gehört auch eine Besichtigung der Schlösser ihres Cousins, König Ludwigs II. von Bayern, zu den vielen Freizeitmöglichkeiten.

Buchtipp: »Elisabeth. Kaiserin wider Willen« von Brigitte Hamann

Antécédents royaux

Une attitude impériale sera acceptée à condition que vous soyez issus d'une famille royale européenne! Car ici, la tradition impériale perdure. C'est en effet en ce lieu que l'impératrice d'Autriche vint passer ses vacances d'été pendant quelque vingt-cinq ans. La maison d'enfance d'Élisabeth – plus connue sous le nom de Sissi – se trouvait juste à côté. Après son mariage, Sissi revint souvent rendre visite à sa famille, ne se lassant jamais de cet endroit enchanteur. Elle était l'hôtesse la plus illustre de l'hôtel bicentenaire et sans doute la cliente la plus appréciée en raison de la vaste escorte qui l'accompagnait. Après son assassinat à Genève, l'hôtel fut rebaptisé Kaiserin Elisabeth en son honneur. Dans le jardin, une statue de l'impératrice se dresse à l'endroit où elle aimait contempler le lac au pied des Alpes.

Le paysage est l'un des grands atouts de l'hôtel, de même que le terrain de golf très réputé. Ceux qui ne souhaitent pas jouer peuvent rester sur la terrasse à lire ou à écrire de la poésie, comme le faisait jadis Sissi. La visite des châteaux construits par ses cousins, notamment Louis II de Bavière, compte parmi les nombreuses excursions à faire dans la région.

Livre à emporter : « Élisabeth d'Autriche » d'Egon César, comte Corti

ANREISE	30 km südlich von München entfernt
PREIS	€€
ZIMMER	65 Zimmer
KÜCHE	Deutsche und österreichische Spezialitäten
GESCHICHTE	Der Gasthof stammt aus dem 19. Jahrhundert und wurde seither mehrmals erweitert und renoviert
X-FAKTOR	Der wunderbare Blick und die romantische Geschichte des Hauses

ACCÈS	À 30 km au sud de Munich
PRIX	€€
CHAMBRES	65 chambres
RESTAURATIONS	Spécialités allemandes et autrichiennes
HISTOIRE	Construit au XIXe siècle, l'hôtel a été agrandi et rénové plusieurs fois
LES « PLUS »	Vue romantique et contexte historique

Lakeside Laze...
Der Seehof, Goldegg am See

Der Seehof, Goldegg am See

Lakeside Laze

Nestled in the pristine natural landscape of the Salzkammer-gut, the Seehof with its stunning views looks down onto a small bog lake. The private area is surrounded by loungers for sunbathing and swimming, but a rowing boat is also available. The charm of the area and thus of the Seehof consists in a skillful combination of tradition-conscious quality and a decisive commitment to contemporaneity. Artists and actors are frequent guests. Literature readings with well-known actors (e. g. the Vienna Burgtheater) take place. The Blue Salon offers a unique library of German literature. But selected newspapers and magazines are, of course, also available. For in-depth reading there is the on-site "Austro Magnum" bar-lounge. Sturdy old chestnut trees shelter the terrace which provides a view of the panoramic mountain scenery and the lake. In the warmer months, all meals of the day from breakfast on can be taken out here – quite a few guests spend most of their vacation here, interrupted only by a trip down to the lake. There are beautiful walks through the woods. But even longer excursions from pasture to pasture are possible. An 18-hole golf course is located in the immediate vicinity, only 1 km away. Those arriving in the cross-country season will, at twilight, appreciate the fireplace indoors. Signposted trails lead deep into the beautiful surrounding countryside. What more do you need? Or, as one journalist put it: "Hotel is perhaps not the right word for this place. We will think of a new one. A place of enchantment, perhaps?"

Book to pack: "Gargoyles" by Thomas Bernhard

Der Seehof
Hofmark 8
485,622 Goldegg am See
Austria
Tel: + 43 (0) 6415 81 37 0
Fax: + 43 (0) 6415 82 76
E-mail: office@derseehof.at
Website: www.derseehof.at

DIRECTIONS	60 km south-west from Salzburg airport and 220 km south-west of Munich airport
RATES	€€
ROOMS	28 rooms, each room individually designed
FOOD	The Restaurant Hecht! r120 has been awarded two toques, and serves local and seasonal produce at the highest level, conjured up into light and inventive menus by the young team led by Sepp Schellhorn
HISTORY	First mentioned as an inn in 1927. Managed by Sepp pand Susi Schellhorn since 1996, in the fifth generation
X-FACTOR	In the summer there's the bog lake with private bathing jetty and rowing boat. In winter, ice skating or cross-country skiing is just on the doorstep. Pure nature!

Chillen am See

Eingebettet in die unberührte Naturlandschaft des Salzkammergutes, erhebt sich der Seehof mit herrlichem Blick über einem kleinen Moorsee. Der hauseigene Steg lädt mit Liegestühlen zum Sonnenbad und Schwimmen ein, aber auch ein Ruderboot liegt dort bereit. Der Reiz der Gegend und so auch des Seehofes besteht in einer gekonnten Verbindung aus Traditionsbewusstsein und entschiedenem Bekenntnis zur Zeitgenossenschaft. Künstler und Schauspieler sind häufige Gäste. Es finden Literaturlesungen mit bekannten Schauspielern (beispielsweise des Wiener Burgtheaters) statt. Der blaue Salon hat eine einzigartige Bibliothek deutschsprachiger Literatur zu bieten. Aber freilich liegen auch ausgewählte Tageszeitungen und Zeitschriften bereit. Zur eingehenden Lektüre bietet sich die hauseigene Bar Austro Magnum an.

Alte, kraftspendende Kastanienbäumen bergen die Terrasse, die den Blick frei gibt auf das Panorama der Berglandschaft mit dem See. In der warmen Jahreszeit können hier vom Frühstück an sämtliche Mahlzeiten des Tages eingenommen werden – nicht wenige Gäste verbringen, nur unterbrochen von einem Gang hinunter zum See, den Großteil ihres Ferienaufenthaltes dort. Sehr schöne Spazierwege führen durch den Wald. Aber auch längere Wanderungen, die dann von Alm zu Alm geführt werden, sind möglich. Ein 18-Loch-Golfplatz befindet sich in unmittelbarer Nachbarschaft, nur 1 km entfernt. Wer in der Langlaufsaison anreist, wird zur Dämmerstunde den Kamin im Haus zu schätzen wissen. Gespurte Loipen führen tief in das wunderschöne Umland hinein. Was braucht man mehr? Oder wie ein Journalist es formulierte: »Hotel ist vielleicht nicht das richtige Wort für diesen Ort. Wir werden ein neues finden. Verzauberungsanstalt vielleicht?«

Buchtipp: »Verstörung« von Thomas Bernhard

Douceur de vivre au bord du lac

Au cœur de la nature préservée de la Salzkammergut, le Seehof a une vue magnifique sur le petit étang marécageux qu'il domine. Le ponton de l'hôtel et ses chaises-longues invitent irrésistiblement aux bains de soleil et aux baignades, mais une barque y est aussi amarrée. Le charme de la région, et aussi du Seehof, réside dans le mariage parfait entre tradition délibérée et appartenance volontaire à l'époque contemporaine. Les clients comptent de nombreux artistes et acteurs. Des lectures littéraires sont organisées avec la participation d'acteurs célèbres (notamment du Wiener Burgtheater). Le Salon bleu offre une bibliothèque de littérature allemande absolument unique. Sans oublier, bien sûr, une sélection de quotidiens et magazines. Pour se plonger dans la lecture, le bar « Austro Magnum » est l'endroit idéal.

De vieux marronniers à la force généreuse abritent la terrasse à la vue panoramique dégagée sur les montagnes et le lac. Aux mois les plus chauds de l'année, tous les repas peuvent y être pris, à commencer par le petit déjeuner, et les clients sont nombreux à y passer le plus clair de leur séjour, ne s'interrompant que pour descendre vers le lac. La forêt est parcourue de très jolis sentiers de promenade, mais des randonnées plus longues peuvent aussi être envisagées et se poursuivent alors d'alpage en alpage. Un terrain de golf de 18 trous se trouve à proximité immédiate, à seulement 1 km. Et les amateurs de ski de fond apprécieront la cheminée au crépuscule. Des pistes sont tracées jusque loin dans les environs splendides. Que demander de plus ? Un journaliste l'a formulé par ces mots : « Hôtel n'est peut-être pas le terme approprié pour ce lieu. Nous devons en trouver un autre. Pourquoi pas établissement d'enchantement ? »

Livre à emporter : « Perturbation » de Thomas Bernhard

ANREISE	60 km südwestlich vom Flughafen Salzburg und 220 km südwestlich vom Flughafen München
PREIS	€€
ZIMMER	28 Zimmer, jedes Zimmer ist individuell gestaltet
KÜCHE	Im Restaurant Hecht! r120, mit zwei Hauben ausgezeichnet, werden lokale und saisonale Produkte auf höchstem Niveau von dem jungen Team um Sepp Schellhorn zu leichten und unverkrampften Menüs gezaubert
GESCHICHTE	1927 erstmals urkundlich als Gasthof erwähnt, seit 1996 in der 5. Generation von Sepp und Susi Schellhorn geführt
X-FAKTOR	Moorbadesee mit hauseigenem Badesteg und Ruderboot, im Winter Schlittschuhlaufen oder Skilanglauf vor der Tür

ACCÈS	À 60 km au sud-ouest de l'aéroport de Salzbourg et à 220 km au sud-ouest de l'aéroport de Munich
PRIX	€€
CHAMBRES	28 chambres, chacune conçue individuellement
RESTAURATION	Le restaurant Hecht! r120 est distingué par deux toques. Des produits locaux et de saison sont transformés en menus légers et décontractés de très haut niveau par une équipe jeune autour de Sepp Schellhorn
HISTOIRE	Auberge attestée depuis 1927. Dirigée depuis 1996 par Sepp et Susi Schellhorn, la cinquième génération
LES « PLUS »	Baignades dans le lac marécageux depuis le ponton de l'hôtel et promenades en barque. En hiver, patinage ou ski de fond

EINGANG

Nature, No Ornament...
Hotel Alpenhof Kreuzberg Looshaus, Payerbach

Hotel Alpenhof Kreuzberg Looshaus, Payerbach

Nature, No Ornament

"Design a country house for me; rustic, but with style", might have been the brief that Paul Khuner gave the famous architect Adolf Loos.

This is the house that was built for him in 1930. Loos was keen on design that was free of decoration, and explained his beliefs in an essay titled "Ornament and Crime". He argued that rich materials and good workmanship made up for a lack of decoration, and in fact far outshone it. The house may not be a decorative one, but it is not plain. Kept preserved much like it was when first built, it is now a hotel. The Alpenhof Kreuzberg Looshaus is perched high on a hillside in the Austrian Alps, encircled by fresh clean mountain air. While its function has altered, the present owners have guarded its original nature, which is as it should be for a building that has been recognized as a state treasure. Although some renovation has been carried out, it is in accord with the design. The colourful interior is proof of the architect's edict that planning should be done from the inside out, and his fondness for cubic shapes is obvious. The region is famed for its winter sports and spas, as well as being home to this design jewel.

Books to pack: "Ornament and Crime" by Adolf Loos
"Brother of Sleep" by Robert Schneider

Hotel Alpenhof Kreuzberg Looshaus
Kreuzberg 60
2650 Payerbach
Austria
Tel: + 43 (0) 2666 52911
Fax: + 43 (0) 2666 5291134
E-mail: steiner@looshaus.at
Website: www.looshaus.at

DIRECTIONS	An hour's drive south of Vienna
RATES	€
ROOMS	14 rooms
FOOD	Renowned home-style cooking with regional specialities
HISTORY	Built in 1930, the Looshaus was adapted as a holiday resort at the beginning of the 1950s
X-FACTOR	Design classic in a spectacular setting

Natur, keine Ornamente

»Entwerfen Sie mir ein Landhaus, rustikal, aber mit Stil«, so mag die Anweisung des Lebensmittelfabrikanten Paul Khuner an den berühmten Architekten Adolf Loos gelautet haben.

Das Ergebnis ist dieses 1930 erbaute Haus. Loos war Verfechter eines geradlinigen, schnörkellosen Stils, der seine Philosophie in einem Essay mit dem viel sagenden Titel »Ornament und Verbrechen« erläuterte. Seiner Meinung nach waren hochwertige Materialien und handwerkliches Können weitaus wichtiger als dekorative Elemente. Und so ist dieses zweigeschossige Blockhaus, das bei seiner Umgestaltung zu dem heutigen Hotel weitgehend im Originalzustand belassen wurde, auch nicht überschwänglich ausgeschmückt, dabei jedoch alles andere als schlicht. Das Hotel Alpenhof Kreuzberg Looshaus liegt an einem Berghang hoch in den österreichischen Alpen, umgeben von frischer, reiner Bergluft. Obwohl es seine Funktion geändert hat, haben die heutigen Besitzern es originalgetreu renoviert, wie es einem Gebäude angemessen ist, das als nationales Baudenkmal anerkannt wurde. Notwendige Renovierungsarbeiten erfolgten in engem Einklang mit dem ursprünglichen Design. Die farbenfrohen Interieurs sind der beste Beweis dafür, dass ein Haus von innen nach außen geplant werden sollte, so wie es der Architekt forderte, und zeugen von seiner Liebe zu kubischen Formen.

Abgesehen von diesem architektonischen Juwel ist die Region berühmt für ihr Wintersportangebot und ihre Kurorte.

Buchtipps: »Ornament und Verbrechen« von Adolf Loos »Schlafes Bruder« von Robert Schneider

Nature sans ornements

« Dessinez-moi une maison de campagne, rustique, mais qui ait du style ! » Telle aurait pu être la commande passée par Paul Khuner au célèbre architecte Adolf Loos, et telle est la maison construite pour lui en 1930.

Loos préconisait une architecture dépouillée et a exposé ses principes dans un manifeste intitulé « Ornement et Crime ». Il affirmait que la richesse des matériaux et la qualité du travail compensaient l'absence de décoration, qu'en fait, ces deux facteurs jouaient un rôle bien plus important. Si la maison n'est pas décorative, elle sort cependant de l'ordinaire. Transformée en hôtel, elle conserve en grande partie son état d'origine.

L'Alpenhof Kreuzberg Looshaus, perché à flanc de montagne dans les Alpes autrichiennes, respire l'air frais alpin. Bien qu'il ait changé de fonction, devenant hôtel, ses propriétaires actuels ont veillé à lui garder son aspect original, comme il se doit pour un bâtiment classé. Les quelques rénovations effectuées s'accordent avec la conception d'origine.

L'aménagement aux couleurs vives illustre parfaitement la prédilection de l'architecte pour les formes cubiques et son principe selon lequel la conception devait se faire de l'intérieur.

Outre pour ce bijou d'architecture, la région est réputée pour ses stations de sports d'hiver et ses villes d'eau.

Livre à emporter : « Frère sommeil » de Robert Schneider

ANREISE	Eine Fahrstunde mit dem Auto südlich von Wien
PREIS	€
ZIMMER	14 Zimmer
KÜCHE	Berühmte Hausmannskost mit regionalen Spezialitäten
GESCHICHTE	1930 erbaut und Anfang der 1950er-Jahre zum Hotel umgebaut
X-FAKTOR	Design-Klassiker in spektakulärer Umgebung

ACCÈS	À une heure de route au sud de Vienne
PRIX	€
CHAMBRES	14 chambres
RESTAURATION	Cuisine familiale réputée avec spécialités régionales
HISTOIRE	Construit en 1930, le Looshaus a été transformé en hôtel au début des années 1950
LES « PLUS »	Design classique dans un cadre spectaculaire

End of the Road...
Hotel Belvédère, Wengen

Hotel Belvédère, Wengen

End of the Road

No road leads here, the only way to reach this Swiss village is by mountain railway. However, there are some who won't be disheartened by this fact. If you are here in September, you can watch them run into town; as competitors in what must be one of the most gruelling marathons in the world. The runners pass through Wengen, on their way to even greater heights. In January, athletes in the Downhill Ski Racing World Cup head the opposite way.

Those of us who are not in such a hurry can stay put at the Belvédère Hotel. Rather than run up or ski down the mountains, you can look out at them from the balconies. The charming hotel was built in 1912, and has been kept in its *art nouveau* style. It is in the centre of the lively village, and skiing, hiking, and mountaineering routes are all easily accessible.

As well as the great views, the advantage of the place is that there is little time wasted before setting ski to snow. This is a perfect starting point for several ski runs, most of which lead back to the village; as well as miles of ski pistes there are paths for walkers, and cable cars that take passengers to other picturesque villages.

Book to pack: "The Magic Mountain" by Thomas Mann

Hotel Belvédère

Familie Zinnert

3823 Wengen

Switzerland

Tel: + 41 (0) 33 856 68 68

Fax: + 41 (0) 33 856 68 69

E-mail: hotel@belvedere-wengen.ch

Website: www.belvedere-wengen.ch

DIRECTIONS	Wengen is about 70 km south of Bern. From Interlaken by rail to Lauterbrunnen and then to Wengen. The hotel is five minutes walk from the Wengen train station
RATES	€
ROOMS	62 rooms
FOOD	Bracing classic Swiss fare served in the hotel's restaurant. Nearby is the Piz Gloria, a revolving restaurant 3,000 m up, on the top of one of the highest peaks in Europe
HISTORY	The Belvédère was built 1912 in the *art nouveau* style
X-FACTOR	Character hotel in a resort village that have both kept their charm

Am Ende der Straße

Es gibt keine Straße, sondern nur eine Bergbahn, mit der Sie dieses schweizerische Dorf erreichen können. Doch einige Leute scheinen diese Tatsache zu ignorieren. Im September kann man ihnen dabei zusehen, wie sie in die Stadt rennen, genauer gesagt, wie sie an einem der anstrengendsten Marathonläufe der Welt teilnehmen. Die Läufer passieren Wengen, bevor sie noch größere Höhen erklimmen müssen. Im Januar aber rasen die Sportler beim World Cup im Abfahrtslauf in genau die entgegengesetzte Richtung.

Wer jedoch keine solche Eile hat, kann einfach im Hotel Belvédère bleiben. Anstatt die Berge hinaufzurennen oder herabzudonnern, kann man sie vom Balkon aus einfach nur genießen. Das charmante Hotel stammt aus dem Jahr 1912; seine Jugendstil-Architektur wurde bis heute erhalten. Mitten im Zentrum des äußerst lebendigen Skiortes gelegen, lässt es sich direkt vor der Haustür natürlich auch Ski fahren, wandern oder bergsteigen.

Abgesehen vom wunderschönen Panorama hat Wengen noch einen anderen großen Pluspunkt. Skiläufer müssen keine langen Wege auf sich nehmen, sondern gelangen schnell zu mehreren Pisten, von denen die meisten ins Dorf zurückführen. Außerdem gibt es Wanderwege sowie Gondeln, die sie zu anderen, nicht minder pittoresken Dörfern und wieder zurückbringen.

Buchtipp: »Der Zauberberg« von Thomas Mann

Le bout du monde

Il n'y a pas de route pour s'y rendre ; seul un petit train de montagne permet d'accéder à ce village suisse. Mais certains ne l'utilisent même pas : si vous séjournez ici en septembre, vous verrez une foule pressée avancer vers la ville, dans le cadre de ce qui doit être l'un des plus rudes marathons du monde. Les coureurs traversent Wengen avant de s'élancer dans les hauteurs. En janvier, les athlètes de la Coupe du monde de ski alpin dévalent dans l'autre sens.

Les moins sportifs, quant à eux, choisiront de loger à l'Hôtel Belvédère. Plutôt que de gravir les montagnes ou les descendre à ski, ils observeront les champions depuis leur balcon. Ce charmant hôtel de style Art nouveau, construit en 1912, est situé au centre du village animé. Il se prête à toutes les activités de montagne, ski, randonnée et alpinisme.

Outre un superbe panorama, le Belvédère offre un accès direct aux pistes de ski, dont la plupart rejoignent le village. En plus des kilomètres de pistes, on trouvera également de beaux sentiers de randonnée et des téléphériques menant à d'autres localités pittoresques des environs.

Livre à emporter : « La Montagne magique » de Thomas Mann

ANREISE	Wengen liegt etwa 70 km südlich von Bern. Mit dem Zug erreichen Sie Wengen von Interlaken über Lauterbrunnen. Vom Bahnhof sind es nur fünf Minuten zu Fuß zum Hotel
PREIS	€
ZIMMER	62 Zimmer
KÜCHE	Klassische schweizerische Küche im Hotelrestaurant. In der Nähe liegt in 3 000 m Höhe, auf einem der höchsten Gipfel Europas, das Drehrestaurant Piz Gloria
GESCHICHTE	Das Belvédère wurde 1912 im Jugendstil erbaut
X-FAKTOR	Individuelles Hotel in einem Erholungsort – beide mit großem Charme

ACCÈS	À environ 70 km au sud de Berne. En train depuis Interlaken via Lauterbrunnen ; l'hôtel est à 5 minutes à pied de la gare de Wengen
PRIX	€
CHAMBRES	62 chambres
RESTAURATION	Le restaurant de l'hôtel sert de solides spécialités suisses. À proximité, le Piz Gloria est un restaurant panoramique situé à 3 000 m d'altitude
HISTOIRE	L'hôtel de style Art nouveau a été construit en 1912
LES « PLUS »	Hôtel de caractère dans une station de sports d'hiver de charme

On Top of the World...
Badrutt's Palace Hotel, St. Moritz

Badrutt's Palace Hotel, St. Moritz

On Top of the World

This grand old hotel is as much a symbol of St. Moritz as are the mountains and the lake. In the late 19th century, the original owners are credited with creating what were then brand new winter sports. Before that time, travellers came to the Alps much more in summer; to hike across the hillsides, see the wildflowers and the massive peaks. By building the world's first toboggan run, and a curling rink, the proprietor lured guests to stay at his hotel in the midst of cold weather. The Palace Hotel, with its tower and memorable silhouette, has become a landmark building. Set in splendid and still unspoiled scenery, this is an institution in the best sense of the word. Life is peaceful here, in spite of being at the centre of this highly social resort. Skiing, polo, and horse races on the snow are part of its appeal, as is the climate. St. Moritz boasts that the sun shines here on an average of 322 days a year. In fact, the town's style and name became one so well-liked that it has been registered as a trademark. The brand 'St. Moritz; top of the world' sums up both its location and its status.

Book to pack: "Into Thin Air: A Personal Account of the Mount Everest Disaster" by Jon Krakauer

Badrutt's Palace Hotel
Via Serlas 27
7500 St. Moritz
Switzerland
Tel: + 41 (0) 81 837 10 00
Fax: + 41 (0) 81 837 29 99
E-mail: reservations@badruttspalace.com
Website: www.badruttspalace.com

DIRECTIONS	220 km/137 m southeast from Zurich. The train route through the Grisons to the Engadine is one of the most interesting and picturesque routes of Europe
RATES	€€€
ROOMS	157 rooms, including suites. The hotel is closed from mid-September to early January.
FOOD	Three restaurants at the hotel, including a renowned French dining room
HISTORY	The 19th century building opened as the Palace Hotel in 1896
X-FACTOR	The activity on offer – one of the more daring diversions is the Cresta Run, the famous bobsled course

Auf Berges Spitze

Dieses wunderbare alte Grandhotel ist ein Symbol für St.
Moritz genauso wie die Berge und der See. Den ersten Besitzern wird zugeschrieben, im ausgehenden 19. Jahrhundert
den damals völlig neuen Wintersport eingeführt zu haben.
Vorher kamen die Reisenden eher im Sommer in die Alpen,
wanderten, suchten nach wild wachsenden Blumen und
genossen den Anblick der riesigen Bergspitzen. Durch den
Bau der ersten Rodelbahn und einer Curlinganlage gelang
es, die Gäste auch im tiefsten Winter und bei niedrigsten
Temperaturen zu einem Aufenthalt zu verführen. Heute ist
das Palace Hotel mit seinem Turm und seiner denkwürdigen
Silhouette zu einem Wahrzeichen geworden. In einer atemberaubenden und bis heute unzerstörten Idylle liegend, ist
das Hotel eine Institution, hinter deren Mauern man sich
gerne verstecken mag. Im Gegensatz zum Trubel von St. Moritz
verläuft das Leben hier friedlich. Skifahren, Polospielen und
Pferderennen im Schnee sind die Hauptattraktionen, vom
Klima ganz abgesehen. Denn St. Moritz ist mit durchschnitt-
lich 322 Sonnentagen im Jahr gesegnet. Stil und Name des
Ortes sind so bekannt und beliebt, dass es mittlerweile ein
eingetragenes Markenzeichen gibt. Die Marke »St. Moritz –
Top of the World« bezieht sich dabei nicht nur auf die geo-
grafische Lage, sondern auch auf den Status dieses Ortes.
**Buchtipp: »In eisige Höhen. Das Drama am Mount Everest«
von Jon Krakauer**

Au sommet du monde

Ce vieil hôtel magnifique est un symbole de Saint-Moritz
autant que le lac et les montagnes qui entourent la localité.
À la fin du XIXe siècle, ses premiers propriétaires jouèrent
un rôle primordial dans la création des sports d'hiver.
Jusqu'alors, on villégiaturait surtout en été dans les Alpes,
pour y faire de la randonnée, admirer les fleurs sauvages et
les imposants sommets. En construisant la première piste
de luge du monde, ainsi qu'un terrain de curling, l'hôtelier
attira des clients en plein cœur de l'hiver. Le Palace Hotel,
avec sa tour et sa silhouette unique, est devenu un véritable
monument. Situé dans un cadre aussi splendide qu'intact,
l'hôtel est une véritable institution, au sens noble du terme.
La vie y est paisible, malgré sa situation en plein centre de
cette station très courue. Ski, polo et courses de chevaux
sur la neige font partie de ses atouts, sans oublier le climat :
Saint-Moritz bénéficierait de 322 jours de soleil par an.
La station est si renommée que son nom est devenu une
marque déposée. « Saint-Moritz, top of the world » résume
à la fois sa situation et son standing.
Livre à emporter : « Tragédie à l'Everest » de Jon Krakauer

ANREISE	220 km südöstlich von Zürich entfernt. Die Fahrt durch Graubünden und das Engadin gehört zu den malerischsten und interessanten Routen Europas	ACCÈS	À 220 km au sud-est de Zurich. La ligne de chemin de fer à destination d'Engadine, qui traverse les Grisons, est l'un des trajets les plus pittoresques d'Europe
PREIS	€€€	PRIX	€€€
ZIMMER	157 Zimmer, Suiten eingeschlossen. Von Mitte September bis Anfang Dezember ist das Hotel geschlossen	CHAMBRES	157 chambres, dont plusieurs suites. Fermeture annuelle à la mi-septembre au début de janvier
KÜCHE	Das Hotel verfügt über sechs Restaurants, darunter einen berühmten Dinersaal im französischen Stil	RESTAURATION	L'hôtel compte six restaurants, dont le restaurant français, très réputé
GESCHICHTE	Das Hotel aus dem 19. Jahrhundert eröffnete 1896	HISTOIRE	Construit au XIXe siècle, l'hôtel a ouvert ses portes en 1896
X-FAKTOR	Das Angebot an Aktivitäten. Für den Cresta-Run auf der gleichnamigen Bob-Bahn muss man etwas Mut aufbringen	LES « PLUS »	Les activités proposées, notamment le Cresta Run, célèbre course de bobsleigh

Majestic Seclusion...
Château de Bagnols, Beaujolais

Château de Bagnols,
Beaujolais

Majestic Seclusion

Lord of all you can see – at least this could be your dream, as you look out from the ramparts of what was once a fortress, and now is a secluded retreat.

Complete with moat and drawbridge, the Château de Bagnols stands on a high vantage point in the lovely Burgundy countryside, guarding its guests from the public gaze and cares of the outside world. Hidden behind massive stone buttresses and towers are a fabulous hotel and garden, a haven for the fortunate few. First built in 1221 as a medieval stronghold, the Chateau is now one of France's historic monuments, restored to its rightful splendour. Its portcullis opens to reveal peaceful gardens and terraces, sheltered by yew hedges and encircled by a stone wall. After entering the castle's courtyard, the arriving guests step into an atmosphere of history and grandeur. Many of the rooms have striking Renaissance wall paintings, uncovered during recent restoration. Antique beds are hung with period silk velvets and embroideries; rich tapestries adorn walls, and great elaborately carved fireplaces blaze out warmth in the winter.

The famous vineyards of Beaujolais and the charming towns and villages in the rolling green hills and valleys beyond may well tempt you out from your castle realm.

Book to pack: "The Red and the Black" by Stendhal

Château de Bagnols

69620 Bagnols

France

Tel: + 33 (0) 474 71 4000

Fax: + 33 (0) 474 71 4049

E-mail: info@chateaudebagnols.fr

Website: www.chateaudebagnols.com

DIRECTIONS	24 km/15 m north of Lyon
RATES	€€€€
ROOMS	27 rooms, including suites
FOOD	French gastronomic and French bistronomic menu
HISTORY	Built in 1221, the château has been transformed several times over the centuries. The hotel was opened in 1991
X-FACTOR	Regal rural retreat, privacy assured

Majestätische Ruhe

Wenn Sie vom Schutzwall dieser ehemaligen Festung um sich schauen, werden Sie sich wie der Herr über die Ihnen zu Füßen liegenden Ländereien fühlen. Denn das Château de Bagnols, umgeben von einem Graben mit einer Ziehbrücke, überragt majestätisch die liebliche Landschaft des Burgund. Heute birgt es ein abgeschiedenes Plätzchen, das Schutz vor der Außenwelt bietet.

Versteckt hinter massiven steinernen Pfeilern und Türmen befindet sich ein Hotel mit einem wunderschönen Garten, in dem Sie sich herrlich entspannen können. Das im Jahr 1221 errichtete mittelalterliche Château gehört heute zu Frankreichs Baudenkmälern. Hinter seinem Falltor erstrecken sich friedliche Gärten und Terrassen, geschützt durch Eibenhecken und eine steinerne Mauer. Sobald Sie den Burghof betreten, werden Sie von der ganz besonderen Atmosphäre verzaubert. Viele der Zimmer bestechen durch eindrucksvolle Wandgemälde aus der Renaissance, die erst vor kurzem freigelegt wurden. Seidensamtvorhänge und Stickereien zieren die antiken Betten; die Wände sind mit üppigen Gobelins behängt, und große Kamine mit kunstvollen Einfassungen verbreiten im Winter wohlige Wärme. Doch die berühmten Weinberge des Beaujolais sowie die reizenden Städte und Dörfer, die verstreut über die umgebenden Hügel und Täler liegen, sind geschaffen dafür, Sie auch gelegentlich hinter Ihren Burgmauern hervorzulocken.

Buchtipp: »Rot und Schwarz« von Stendhal

Une retraite majestueuse

Montez sur les remparts de cet ancien château fort, aujourd'hui paisible retraite, et imaginez-vous seigneur des lieux qui s'étendent sous votre regard.

Avec ses douves et son pont-levis, le Château de Bagnols, érigé dans une situation admirable, domine la ravissante campagne bourguignonne. Derrière ses tours et contreforts massifs se cachent un hôtel fabuleux et un charmant parc, paradis pour les happy few. Forteresse médiévale dont la construction débute en 1221, ce château classé monument historique a retrouvé sa splendeur d'antan. La herse se lève pour révéler des jardins et terrasses paisibles, abrités derrière des haies d'ifs et entourés d'un mur en pierre. Histoire et splendeur accueillent les hôtes dès leur arrivée dans la cour du château. Un grand nombre des salles sont revêtues de magnifiques fresques Renaissance, découvertes durant la récente restauration. Les lits anciens sont fermés par des rideaux de velours de soie et de dentelles d'époque ; de riches tapisseries ornent les murs et, en hiver, les grandes cheminées sculptées avec art font rayonner leur chaleur.

Les célèbres vignobles du Beaujolais ainsi que les jolis bourgs et villages qui émaillent ce paysage de collines et vallées verdoyantes vous inciteront certainement à quitter les murs de votre château de rêve.

Livre à emporter : « Le Rouge et le Noir » de Stendhal

ANREISE	24 km nördlich von Lyon
PREIS	€€€€
ZIMMER	27 Zimmer, einschließlich Suiten
KÜCHE	Französische Küche und Menüs
GESCHICHTE	Das Gebäude wurde 1221 errichtet und über die Jahrhunderte mehrfach umgebaut. Als Hotel wurde es 1991 eröffnet
X-FAKTOR	Königliches, ländliches Refugium mit garantiertem Schutz der Privatsphäre

ACCÈS	À 24 km au nord de Lyon
PRIX	€€€€
CHAMBRES	27 chambres dont des suites
RESTAURATION	Gastronomie française et menu français bistronomique
HISTOIRE	Construit en 1221, le bâtiment a été transformé plusieurs fois au cours des siècles. L'hôtel a ouvert en 1991
LES « PLUS »	Retraite rurale royale, tranquillité garantie

In Vino Veritas...
Les Sources de Caudalie, Bordeaux-Martillac

Les Sources de Caudalie, Bordeaux-Martillac

In Vino Veritas

A small glass of wine, so the doctor says, is good for the health. Well, here you can enjoy both drinking a nice red or white wine, and also bathe in it. Les Sources de Caudalie is a hotel that flatters the whole palate. Not only does this hotel possess an exceptional spa facility, it also just happens to be in the middle of a vineyard.

Those who would like to indulge in its unique "wine therapy" can try a Merlot wet pack, a Sauvignon massage or a body scrub with crushed Cabernet grape pips. Some of the treatments, whether anti-ageing or weight-loss programs, are based on wine products and taste as good as they look. Moreover, the gourmet is given the choice of three restaurants (one of which has a Michelin star), and a wine cellar with over 15,000 bottles of excellent wines. In the French Paradox bar you can spoil your taste buds with tastings of special vintages, and these can also be enjoyed in the so-called Tasting Tower with beautiful views of the surrounding area. And if you're not actually visiting the restaurant or the spa, you can, for example, take tours by bike or limousine to the nearby major wineries of the Médoc, Sauternes, Pomerol and Saint-Émilion regions. Departure is sweetened not only by souvenirs of local wine production, but also by Caudalie's grape-based skin-care series.

Book to pack: "Le Grand Meaulnes" by Alain-Fournier

Les Sources de Caudalie
Chemin de Smith Haut-Lafitte
33650 Bordeaux-Martillac
France
Tel: + 33 (0) 557 838 383
Fax: + 33 (0) 557 838 384
E-mail: sources@sources-caudalie.com
Website: www.sources-caudalie.com

DIRECTIONS	15 minutes south from Bordeaux
RATES	€€
ROOMS	61 rooms and suites
FOOD	A veritable feast for the senses awaits you
HISTORY	Les Sources de Caudalie were built and opened in 1999
X-FACTOR	Wine treats for palate, senses and body

Im Wein liegt Wahrheit

Ein Gläschen Wein, so sagt der Hausarzt, sei gut für die Gesundheit. Hier können Sie nicht nur einen guten Rot- oder Weißwein trinken, Sie können auch in ihm baden. Les Sources de Caudalie ist ein Hotel, das rundherum dem Gaumen schmeichelt. Nicht nur, dass dieses Hotel eine außergewöhnliche Wellnessanlage besitzt, es liegt zudem zufälligerweise mitten in einem Weinberg.

Wer sich mit der einzigartigen »Vinotherapie« verwöhnen lassen möchte, kann einen Merlotwickel versuchen, eine Sauvignonmassage oder ein Körperpeeling mit zerstoßenen Cabernettraubenkernen. Einige der Behandlungen, ob Anti-Age oder Abnehmkur, basieren auf Weinprodukten und schmecken so gut, wie sie aussehen. Überdies werden dem Feinschmecker gleich drei Restaurants (eines davon besitzt einen Michelin Stern) und ein Weinkeller mit über 15 000 Flaschen exzellenter Tropfen geboten. In der Bar French Paradox werden ihre Geschmacksnerven mit Kostproben besonderer Jahrgänge verwöhnt, diese kann man auch in dem sogenannten Tasting Tower mit schönen Ausblicken auf die Umgebung genießen.

Und wenn Sie nicht gerade das Restaurant oder den Wellnessbereich besuchen, können Sie zum Beispiel Touren per Fahrrad oder Limousine zu den nahe gelegenen bedeutenden Weingütern der Regionen des Médoc, Sauternes, Pomerol und Saint-Émilion unternehmen. Der Abschied schließlich lässt sich nicht nur durch Mitbringsel der örtlichen Weinproduktion versüßen, sondern auch durch Caudalies Hautpflegeserie auf Traubenbasis.

Buchtipp: »Der große Meaulnes« von Alain-Fournier

La vérité est dans le vin

Un petit verre de vin serait bon pour la santé, tous les médecins le disent. Ici, vous ne vous contenterez pas de déguster un bon rouge ou blanc, vous pourrez aussi vous y baigner. Les Sources de Caudalie est un hôtel où tout flatte le palais. Avec son centre de bien-être particulièrement original, il est situé comme par hasard au cœur d'un vignoble.

Pour vous faire choyer par la « vinothérapie » unique en son genre, vous aurez le choix entre un enveloppement merlot, un massage au sauvignon ou un peeling corps au cabernet concassé. Certains des soins, anti-âge ou minceur, sont basés sur des produits du vin et sont aussi bons à déguster qu'à voir. Les gourmets ont par ailleurs le choix entre trois restaurants (dont un avec une étoile au Michelin) et une cave de plus de 15 000 bouteilles de choix. Au bar French Paradox, les papilles sont particulièrement soignées avec des dégustations de grands millésimes, à apprécier depuis la « Tasting Tower » et les belles vues sur le paysage.

Et quand vous ne serez ni au restaurant, ni dans l'espace bien-être, vous pourrez faire des tours en vélo ou en limousine jusqu'aux grands domaines tout proches du Médoc, de Sauternes, Pomerol et Saint-Émilion. Pour finir, les adieux seront moins amers avec un souvenir de la production viticole locale, mais aussi la série de soins pour la peau Caudalie à base de raisin.

Livre à emporter : « Le Grand Meaulnes » d'Alain-Fournier

ANREISE	15 Minuten südlich von Bordeaux		ACCÈS	À 15 minutes au sud de Bordeaux
PREIS	€€		PRIX	€€
ZIMMER	61 Zimmer und Suiten		CHAMBRES	61 chambres et suites
KÜCHE	Ein wahres Fest für die Sinne		RESTAURATION	Le nec plus ultra pour les sens
GESCHICHTE	Erbaut und eröffnet 1999		HISTOIRE	Construit et ouvert en 1999
X-FAKTOR	Wein für Gaumen, Sinne und Körper		LES « PLUS »	Du vin pour le goût, la santé, la beauté

Joie de Vivre...
Les Prés d'Eugénie, Landes

Les Prés d'Eugénie, Landes

Joie de Vivre

For some, this is a place of pilgrimage. Those who value fine dining come here to savour the great food and wine, devised by one of France's most well-known chefs. This is Michel Guérard's resort, where the ambience is as delicious as the food. Les Prés d'Eugénie are a cluster of hotels, restaurants, and a health spa. They have been described as being the model for what a country retreat should be like. Indeed, this is the image of the good life. Guests are treated to a blend of herb gardens and climbing roses, exotic fragrances and delicious flavours, exquisite guestrooms, and sparkling springs. The mixing of such fine ingredients makes this a very inviting setting. The old adage that two cooks are better than one does not apply here. Michel reigns over the cuisine, and his wife Christine has created the rest. The buildings, gardens, and the spa are her realm, while the restaurant is a national treasure, in a country that is famous for its food.

The resort is in the village of Eugénie-les-Bains, in the heart of the Landes forest. It is a town so picturesque that it almost looks like a movie set.

Book to pack: "How Proust Can Change Your Life" by Alain de Botton

Les Prés d'Eugénie

40320 Eugénie-les-Bains
Landes
France
Tel : + 33 (0) 558 050 607
Fax : + 33 (0)558 511 010
E-mail: reservation@michelguerard.com
Website: www.michelguerard.com

DIRECTIONS	Les Prés d'Eugénie are located in the village of Eugénie-les-Bains, in the heart of the Aquitaine Region. Pau Airport is 45 km/28 m away, Bordeaux Airport is 120 km/74 m north
RATES	€€€
ROOMS	45 rooms and apartments
FOOD	The raison d'être
HISTORY	Les Prés d'Eugénie were built in the 18th century and opened in 1862 as hotel
X-FACTOR	The art of living and eating

Joie de vivre

Wer gute Küche zu schätzen weiß, der kommt hierher, um hervorragendes Essen und große Weine zu genießen. Sie werden kredenzt von Michel Guérard, einem der bekanntesten Köche des Landes, der hier seinen Wirkungsort hat. Das Ambiente des Hotels steht jedoch dem Essen in seiner »Köstlichkeit« in nichts nach. Les Prés d'Eugénie ist ein Ensemble aus mehreren Hotels, Restaurants und einer Wellnessanlage. Auf ideale Weise wird einem hier ein ruhiges Leben auf dem Land, ein Sinnbild für das Leben, wie es sein sollte, geboten. Der Gast wird verwöhnt mit duftenden Kräutergärten und rankenden Rosen, exotischen Düften und köstlichen Aromen, exquisiten Gästezimmern und perlenden Quellen. Die perfekte Mischung dieser Zutaten macht den Ort so einladend. Dass viele Köche den Brei verderben, nun, das weiß Michel Guérard. Deshalb hat er die Oberhoheit über die Küche, und seine Frau Christine gestaltet den Rest der Anlage. Gebäude, Gärten und die Wellnessanlage sind ihr Reich, das Restaurant aber ist ein nationales Heiligtum. Die Hotelanlage liegt in dem malerischen Örtchen Eugénie-les-Bains, im Herzen der Wälder der Landes. Hier ist es so pittoresk, dass man sich in einer Spielfilmkulisse zu befinden glaubt.

Buchtipp: »Wie Proust Ihr Leben verändern kann« von Alain de Botton

Joie de vivre

Les amateurs de bonne chère viennent ici déguster d'excellents vins et une délicieuse cuisine concoctée par l'un des chefs les plus réputés de France. C'est le fief de Michel Guérard, et l'ambiance y est à la hauteur de la gastronomie. Les Prés d'Eugénie, qui regroupent plusieurs hôtels et restaurants ainsi qu'un centre thermal, ont été décrits comme un modèle de retraite champêtre. Pour beaucoup d'hôtes, il s'agit même d'un véritable lieu de pèlerinage. Il est vrai que le complexe est l'image même du «bien-être»: on y déambule parmi les plantes aromatiques et les roses grimpantes, les parfums exotiques et les odeurs alléchantes, les salons élégants et les sources d'eau chaude. Le mariage réussi de tous ces ingrédients forme un cadre résolument enchanteur. Michel Guérard règne sur la cuisine, dont l'éloge n'est plus à faire; son épouse Christine s'occupe du reste: résidences, jardins et thermes.

Le complexe hôtelier se trouve à Eugénie-les-Bains, au cœur de la forêt landaise; une petite ville si pittoresque qu'on la croirait créée pour un film.

Livre à emporter: «Comment Proust peut changer votre vie» d'Alain de Botton

ANREISE	Im Dorf Eugénie-les-Bains im Herzen von Aquitanien gelegen. Der Flughafen von Pau ist 45 km entfernt, der Flughafen von Bordeaux liegt 120 km nördlich von Eugénie-les-Bains
PREIS	€€€
ZIMMER	45 Zimmer und Apartments
KÜCHE	La raison d'être
GESCHICHTE	Die Gebäude stammen aus dem 18. Jahrhundert. Das Hotel wurde 1862 eröffnet
X-FAKTOR	Die Kunst zu leben und die Kunst zu essen

ACCÈS	Les Prés d'Eugénie sont situés à Eugénie-les-Bains, au centre de l'Aquitaine. L'aéroport de Pau se trouve à 45 km, celui de Bordeaux à 120 km au nord d'Eugénie-les-Bains
PRIX	€€€
CHAMBRES	45 chambres et appartements
RESTAURATION	La raison d'être
HISTOIRE	Construit au XVIIIe siècle, hôtel depuis 1862
LES « PLUS »	L'art de vivre dans toute sa splendeur

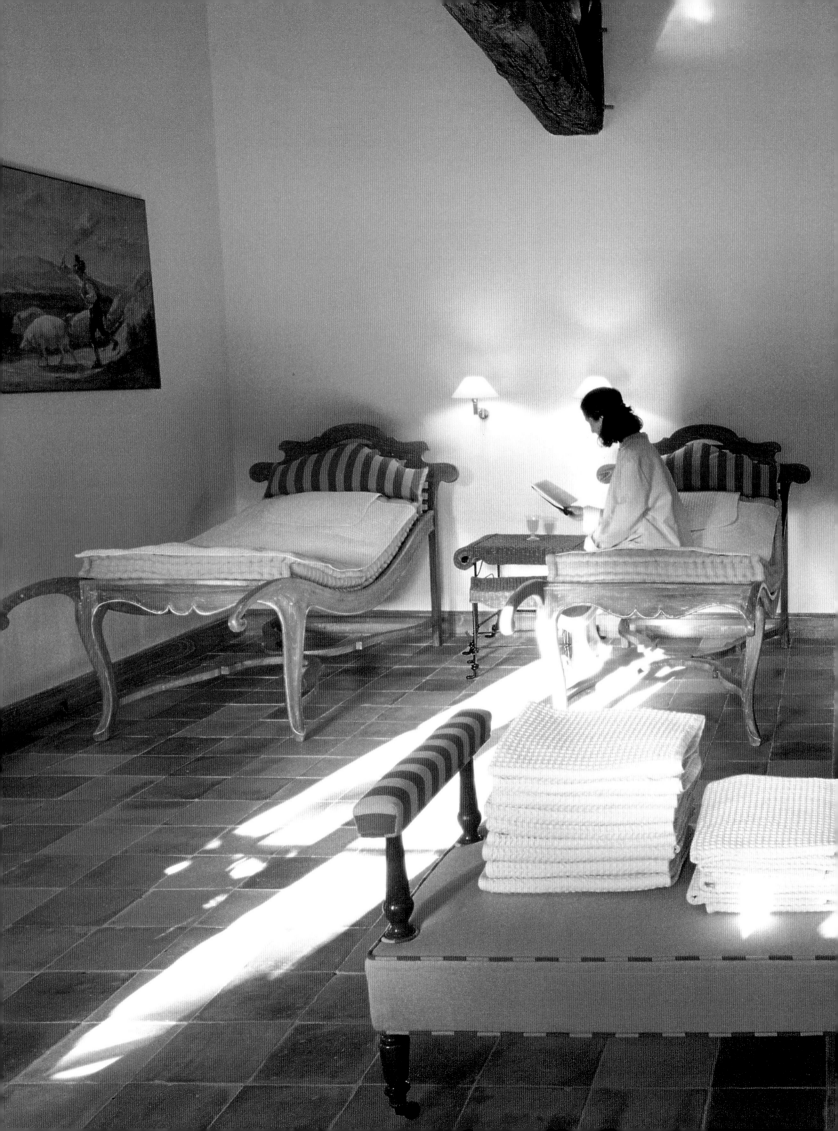

Far from the Madding Crowd...
Les Maisons Marines d'Huchet, Aquitaine

Les Maisons Marines d'Huchet, Aquitaine

Far from the Madding Crowd

A tall structure often marks the site of somewhere special. In a distant place in France, far from the crowds that flock to see his famous Parisian tower, there is a small marine beacon built by Gustave Eiffel. It also marks a special spot. On the Atlantic coast between Bordeaux and Biarritz there are many miles of deserted beaches, edged by forests of pine trees. Hidden amongst the sand dunes is a tiny retreat where the motto is "keep it simple". Les Maisons Marines consist of just three beach houses, an unusual trio. The distinctive main house was built some 150 years ago as a hunting lodge. The other two houses, once boatsheds, are now charming little guest cottages set apart in this quiet hideaway. Access to Les Maisons Marines is circuitous; there is no direct route to here, because first you must stay at one of Michel and Christine Guérard's hotels at Eugénie-les-Bains, like Les Prés d'Eugénie, to gain admittance to the beach houses. They are more like a private home than a hotel, one the owners invite you to share, and a special place to take time out and savour the solitude. The sound of the surf will lull you to sleep.

Book to pack: "Les Misérables" by Victor Hugo

Les Maisons Marines d'Huchet	
40320 Eugénie-les-Bains	
France	
Tel: + 33 (0) 5 58 05 06 07	
Fax: + 33 (0) 5 58 51 10 10	
E-mail: guerard@relaischateaux.fr	
Website: www.relaischateaux.fr/guerard	

DIRECTIONS	150 km/93 m south from Bordeaux Airport
RATES	€€€
ROOMS	2 houses that accommodate two people
FOOD	Menus by a master chef
HISTORY	Built in the middle of the 19th century, Les Maisons Marines opened as guesthouses in December 1999
X-FACTOR	Solitude and scenery with special surroundings and food

Abseits des Massentourismus

Es kommt häufig vor, dass ein Ort, der etwas Außergewöhnliches zu bieten hat, durch ein hohes Bauwerk gekennzeichnet ist. In einem entlegenen Winkel an der Westküste Frankreichs, weitab von den Touristenmassen, die sich um seinen berühmten Turm in Paris drängen, steht ein kleines, von Gustave Eiffel erbautes Leuchtfeuer, das mit Sicherheit auf einen ganz besonderen Ort verweist.

Zwischen Bordeaux und Biarritz erstrecken sich entlang der Atlantikküste lange, einsame Strände, die von Pinienwäldern geschützt werden. Versteckt in den Sanddünen liegt ein kleines Refugium, in dem das Motto »weniger ist mehr« stilvoll gelebt wird. Les Maisons Marines sind genau drei Strandhäuser: Das markante Haupthaus wurde vor etwa 150 Jahren als Jagdhütte erbaut. Die beiden anderen Gebäude dienten früher als Bootshäuser und sind heute bezaubernde kleine Ferienhäuschen, die ganz im Verborgenen liegen. Es ist jedoch ein Umweg nötig, um nach Les Maisons Marines zu kommen, denn Sie müssen zuvor in einem der Hotels von Michel und Christine Guérard in Eugénie-les-Bains, wie etwa dem Les Prés d'Eugénie, zu Gast gewesen sein. In den Strandhäusern sind Sie dann eher privilegierter Hausgast der Besitzer als Hotelbesucher. Nutzen Sie die Abgeschiedenheit, um zur Ruhe zu kommen, und lassen Sie sich nachts vom Rauschen des Meeres in den Schlaf wiegen.

Buchtipps: »Die Elenden« von Victor Hugo

Loin des foules

Il est fréquent qu'un lieu extraordinaire se distingue par un bâtiment de haute taille. Dans un coin reculé de France, loin des foules qui affluent pour visiter la célèbre tour Eiffel à Paris, se trouve un petit phare également construit par Gustave Eiffel, soulignant lui aussi un lieu remarquable.

De Bordeaux à Biarritz, la côte Atlantique s'étend sur des kilomètres de plages désertes, bordées de forêts de pins. Dans les dunes se cache une retraite minuscule où le mot d'ordre est « simplicité ». Au nombre de trois, ces Maisons Marines forment un trio original. La plus grande, d'aspect distinctif, est un ancien pavillon de chasse construit il y a environ 150 ans. Les deux autres, d'anciens hangars à bateaux, sont aujourd'hui de charmantes petites maisons d'hôtes, situées à l'écart dans cette retraite paisible.

L'accès aux Maisons Marines se fait par des chemins détournés : pour y être admis, il faut d'abord séjourner dans l'un des hôtels de Michel et Christine Guérard, à Eugénie-les-Bains ou aux Prés d'Eugénie. Elles ressemblent moins à un hôtel qu'à des demeures privées que leur propriétaire vous aurait invité à partager. Dans ce lieu privilégié dont vous savourerez la solitude, vous vous reposerez, bercé par le clapotis des vagues.

Livre à emporter : « Les Misérables » de Victor Hugo

ANREISE	150 km südlich vom internationalen Flughafen Bordeaux
PREIS	€€€
ZIMMER	2 Häuser für je 2 Personen
KÜCHE	Menüs gekocht von einem Spitzenkoch
GESCHICHTE	Les Maisons Marines wurden Mitte des 19. Jahrhundert erbaut und werden seit Dezember 1999 als Gästehäuser genutzt
X-FAKTOR	Abgeschiedenheit, schöne Umgebung und hervorragendes Essen

ACCÈS	À 150 km au sud de l'aéroport international de Bordeaux
PRIX	€€€
CHAMBRES	2 maisons accueillant deux personnes
RESTAURATION	Cuisine d'un chef cuisinier
HISTOIRE	Construites au milieu du XIXe siècle, Les Maisons Marines ouvraient leurs portes en décembre 1999
LES « PLUS »	Solitude, cadre superbe et gastronomie

Inner Sanctum...
La Mirande, Avignon

La Mirande, Avignon

Inner Sanctum

In medieval times, Avignon was the residence of several popes. Conflicts within the Catholic Church as well as between the Pope and the worldly powers are to be held responsible for this relocation.

The Pope's temporary displacement to Avignon resulted in a building fervour, as cardinals and prelates of the church strove to construct worthy earthly palaces and houses to dwell in. Originally the site of a 14th-century cardinal's residence, La Mirande is blessed with an ideal position. It is in the heart of the city, in a tranquil cobbled square, at the very foot of the Popes' Palace. Behind the hotel's original stone façade is an exquisite interior; one that bears testament to a real quest to attain a near faultless authenticity. Its success is such that even though it is relatively new, the interior seems to have evolved over generations and time.

Meticulously restored, using the style and materials of the 17th and 18th century, La Mirande has all the splendour of an aristocratic residence of the era, together with the best of contemporary cuisine. Under the coffered ceiling of the restaurant, inventive fare that makes you truly grateful is served.

Books to pack: "All Men are Mortal" by Simone de Beauvoir "Tartarin de Tarascon" by Alphonse Daudet

La Mirande		
4, Place de la Mirande		
84000 Avignon		
France		
Tel: + 33 (0) 490 142 020		
Fax: + 33 (0) 490 862 685		
E-mail: mirande@la-mirande.fr		
Website: www.la-mirande.fr		

DIRECTIONS	2.5 hours south from Paris by TGV; in the centre of Avignon
RATES	€€€
ROOMS	25 rooms and 1 suite
FOOD	Provencal and French cuisine, with a cooking school for disciples
HISTORY	Originally built in the 14th century, La Mirande was transformed several times over the centuries. The hotel was opened in 1990
X-FACTOR	Aristocratic interior and heavenly food

Im Allerheiligsten

Im Mittelalter war Avignon mehrfach für kurze Zeit Sitz des Papstes. Konflikte innerhalb der Kurie sowie zwischen Päpsten und weltlichen Mächten führten zu diesen unfreiwilligen Ortswechseln.

Begleitet wurde dieser kurzzeitige Umzug nach Avignon von einem wahren Bauboom, denn Kardinäle und Prälaten der Kirche machten es sich zur Aufgabe, schon auf Erden Paläste und Häuser zu errichten, die ihrer würdig waren. Wo heute das Hotel La Mirande steht, befand sich im 14. Jahrhundert die Residenz eines Kardinals. Auch strategisch liegt das Hotel himmlisch, mitten im Herzen der Stadt nämlich, an einem verträumten Platz mit Kopfsteinpflaster, direkt am Fuß des Papstpalastes. Hinter der Originalfassade des Hotels versteckt sich ein herrliches Interieur, das auf Schritt und Tritt das Bestreben erkennen lässt, so viel Authentizität wie möglich herzustellen. Obwohl noch gar nicht alt, wirkt die Innengestaltung, als hätten an ihr ganze Generationen und Zeitläufte gewirkt.

Im Stil des 17. und 18. Jahrhunderts bis ins Detail restauriert, strahlt La Mirande die Pracht einer aristokratischen Residenz aus und bietet gleichzeitig das Beste aus der heutigen Küche. Unter der Kassettendecke des Restaurants wird kreative Kochkunst geboten, die zu wahren Dankesgebeten verleitet.

Buchtipps: »Alle Menschen sind sterblich« von Simone de Beauvoir

»Die Abenteuer des Herrn Tartarin aus Tarascon« von Alphonse Daudet

Inner sanctum

Au Moyen Âge, Avignon devint pendant plusieurs courtes périodes la ville des Papes, lorsque des conflits au sein de la curie et entre la papauté et les pouvoirs temporels conduisirent à ce changement de résidence involontaire.

L'installation du Pape en Avignon entraîna un boom dans la construction, les cardinaux et prélats rivalisant dans l'édification de palais et demeures luxueuses. Autrefois résidence d'un cardinal du XIVe siècle, l'hôtel La Mirande jouit d'une situation privilégiée. En plein cœur de la ville, sur une paisible place pavée, il se dresse au pied du Palais des Papes. Derrière la façade d'origine, se cache un ravissant intérieur qui se targue de rechercher une authenticité quasi parfaite. Cela avec grand succès, car bien qu'il soit relativement récent, l'intérieur de La Mirande semble avoir évolué au fil des générations et du temps.

Méticuleusement restauré, dans le style et les matériaux des XVIIe et XVIIIe siècles, l'hôtel possède toute la splendeur d'une résidence aristocratique d'époque. S'y ajoute une cuisine contemporaine de grand chef ; sous le plafond à caissons du restaurant, de superbes plats originaux vous seront servis.

Livres à emporter : «Tous les hommes sont mortels» de Simone de Beauvoir

«Aventures prodigieuses de Tartarin de Tarascon» d'Alphonse Daudet

ANREISE	2,5 Stunden Fahrt südlich von Paris mit dem TGV. Im Zentrum von Avignon gelegen	ACCÈS	À 2 heures 30 au sud de Paris en TGV ; en plein centre-ville d'Avignon
PREIS	€€€	PRIX	€€€
ZIMMER	25 Zimmer und 1 Suite	CHAMBRES	25 chambres et 1 suite
KÜCHE	Restaurant mit provenzalischer und französischer Küche. Eine Kochschule ist dem Restaurant angeschlossen	RESTAURATION	Cuisine française et provençale. Cours de cuisine pour les adeptes
GESCHICHTE	Erbaut im 14. Jahrhundert, mehrfach über die Jahrhunderte umgebaut und 1990 als Hotel eröffnet	HISTOIRE	Construit au XIVe siècle, le bâtiment a été transformé plusieurs fois au cours des siècles. L'hôtel a ouvert en 1990
X-FAKTOR	Aristokratisches Interieur und himmlisches Essen	LES « PLUS »	Intérieur aristocratique et cuisine succulente

A Providential Place...

La Bastide de Marie, Ménerbes

La Bastide de Marie, Ménerbes

A Providential Place

To have a centuries-old house with its own vineyard in one of the most beautiful parts of France, in reach of charming villages, has been a dream of many. High in the Lubéron Mountains of Provence, that fantasy can come partly true by staying at La Bastide de Marie, a small inn more like a home than a hotel. Set in a vineyard that produces promising red, white, and rosé Côtes du Lubéron, the rustic old farmhouse has been given a new lease of life. Contemporary restful colours, and the peace and quiet of the setting make this a haven for travellers who crave tranquillity and nourishment of body and mind. With air the scent of lavender, sunlight bathing the walled garden, and delectable food and wine served beside the pool, one could dream of not going home.

On a nearby hillside is the picturesque village of Ménerbes, which may be as far as guests of La Bastide de Marie might want to venture. For those who feel like going further on shopping expeditions, there are lively weekly markets in the surrounding countryside, specializing in collectables from pottery to antiques.

Books to pack: "The Water of the Hills" by Marcel Pagnol
"Perfume" by Patrick Süskind

La Bastide de Marie

64 chemin des Peirelles
84560 Ménerbes
France
Tel: + 33 (0)4 90 72 30 20
Fax: + 33 (0)4 90 72 54 20
E-mail: contact@labastidedemarie.com
Website: www.labastidedemarie.com

DIRECTIONS	An hour's drive north from Marseille Airport, 40 minutes east from the airport of Avignon; 2.5 hours with TGV south from Paris
RATES	€€€€
ROOMS	14 rooms including 6 suites and a roulotte
FOOD	The best of Provencal cuisine
HISTORY	Built in the 18th century, La Bastide de Marie was opened as a hotel in 2000
X-FACTOR	A taste of Provence the way it should be

Ein schicksalhafter Ort

Wer hat nicht schon einmal davon geträumt, Besitzer eines jahrhundertealten Hauses mit eigenem Weinberg zu sein, welches in einer der schönsten Regionen Frankreichs liegt, umgeben von charmanten Dörfern?

Zumindest für eine Weile können Sie sich diesen Traum hoch in den Lubéron-Bergen der Provence in La Bastide de Marie erfüllen, einem bezaubernden, kleinen Hotel, das fast wie ein Zuhause ist. Inmitten eines Weinbergs gelegen, der viel versprechenden roten, weißen und rosé Côtes du Lubéron hervorbringt, erlebt dieses rustikale alte Bauernhaus einen zweiten Frühling. Angenehme, ruhige Farben und die friedliche Umgebung machen es zu einer Zuflucht für Reisende, die sich nach stressfreier Erholung für Körper und Seele sehnen. Wenn Lavendelduft in der Luft liegt, die Sonne auf dem von Mauern geschützten Garten liegt und köstliche Gerichte und Weine am Pool serviert werden, lässt es sich leicht davon träumen, für immer zu bleiben. Auf einem nahe gelegenen Hügel liegt das malerische Dörfchen Ménerbes. Und weiter möchten sich viele Gäste von La Bastide de Marie möglicherweise gar nicht entfernen. Wer aber gern auch mal einen Einkaufsbummel unternimmt, sollte die lebhaften Wochenmärkte in den Dörfern der Umgebung besuchen, wo Sammlerstücke von Töpferwaren bis zu Antiquitäten angeboten werden.

Buchtipps: »Die Wasser der Hügel« von Marcel Pagnol »Das Parfüm« von Patrick Süskind

Un lieu providentiel

Nombreux sont ceux qui rêvent de posséder une vieille maison nichée au coeur des vignes, non loin de charmants villages, dans l'une de ces belles régions de France. Ce rêve se réalise le temps d'un séjour à La Bastide de Marie, une petite auberge perchée dans les Montagnes du Lubéron, qui évoque davantage une maison de famille qu'un hôtel. Située dans un vignoble produisant d'excellents Côtes du Lubéron rouges, blancs et rosés, cette ancienne ferme a trouvé une nouvelle jeunesse. Le décor aux couleurs reposantes et le cadre serein en font un havre de paix pour qui a soif de quiétude et recherche à la fois des nourritures spirituelles et terrestres. Séduit par l'air embaumant la lavande, par le soleil qui baigne le jardin clos et par les mets et vins délicieux servis près de la piscine, on s'imaginerait bien de ne plus jamais rentrer chez soi. Sur une colline voisine s'élève le pittoresque village de Ménerbes. Parfois, les hôtes de La Bastide de Marie ne souhaitent pas s'aventurer plus loin. Les marchés hebdomadaires des environs offrent toutes sortes d'objets, des faïences aux antiquités.

Livre à emporter : « Manon des sources » de Marcel Pagnol « Le Parfum » de Patrick Süskind

ANREISE	1 Fahrstunde nördlich vom Flughafen Marseille, 40 Minuten nach Osten vom Flughafen Avignon; 2,5 Stunden Fahrt südlich von Paris mit dem TGV
PREIS	€€€€
ZIMMER	14 Zimmer, 6 Suiten und ein luxuriöser Wohnwagen
KÜCHE	Das Beste aus der provenzalischen Küche
GESCHICHTE	Im 18. Jahrhundert erbaut, 2000 als Hotel eröffnet
X-FAKTOR	Die Provence von ihrer Glanzseite

ACCÈS	À une heure de route au nord de l'aéroport de Marseille, à 40 minutes à l'est de l'aéroport d'Avignon. À 2 heures 30 au sud de Paris en TGV
PRIX	€€€€
CHAMBRES	14 chambres dont 6 suites et une roulotte
RESTAURATION	Le meilleur de la cuisine provençale
HISTOIRE	Construite au XVIIIe, La Bastide de Marie est un hôtel depuis 2000
LES « PLUS »	La Provence authentique

Vivid Colours of Provence...
Le Cloître, Arles

Le Cloître, Arles

Vivid Colours of Provence

Le Cloître is not only centrally located in Arles, in a peaceful part town; it is also uniquely beautiful in its decor. The Swiss patron of the arts Maja Hoffmann, who owns the hotel, commissioned the Franco-Lebanese architect India Mahdavi to carry out the renovation and furnishing of the historic building. No expense has been spared on furnishings, which makes the cost of rooms all the more amazing. Hand-stitched linen and velvet curtains, custom-made furniture such as sofas, wardrobes and room dividers in combination with selected pieces of furniture by the Bouroullec brothers, Gio Ponti, and the workshops of Vittorio Bonacina adorn the rooms, with their flood of sunlight. India Mahdavi herself has contributed many original solitaires: her marble table "Bishop" is reminiscent of a chess piece; the motif is repeated in a basin of white glazed ceramic, which ensures that you are in a good mood even when you have your morning wash. The special light of Arles had already lured Vincent Van Gogh and Paul Gauguin into the town, which nowadays is famous for its annual Festival of Contemporary Photography. The decisive color design in Le Cloître reminds one very pleasantly of this marriage of light and creativity. Then there is the location of the house: From the roof terrace, the view extends over the Saint Trophime cathedral to the Roman theatre. The Fondation Vincent van Gogh, launched in 2014 by the Swiss pharmaceutical entrepreneurs Hoffmann-LaRoche, is just a short walk away. The museum promotes the engagement of living artists with Van Gogh's work. Maja Hoffmann is the President of the Foundation. The Restaurant La Chassagnette, a little further out in the Camargue, also belongs to Maja Hoffmann. Here all the vegetables and herbs are grown in the organic garden belonging to the restaurant. This short excursion is a must during a stay in Arles.

Book to pack: "Fiesta" by Ernest Hemingway

Hotel du Cloître

18, rue du Cloître

13200 Arles

France

Tel: + 33 (0) 4 88 09 10 00

E-mail: contact@hotel-cloitre.com

www.hotelducloitre.com

DIRECTIONS	45 minutes north of Marseille airport or 20 minutes from the airport or train station in Avignon. 30 min from the TGV train station in Nîmes
RATES	€
ROOMS	19 rooms: 11 double rooms, 2 single rooms, 1 superior, 5 suites
FOOD	There is only breakfast available, all products are local and organically farmed. The restaurant La Chassagnette 30 min outside of Arles has one Michelin star
HISTORY	Parts of the building date from the 13th century, which was newly opened as a hotel in 2012
X-FACTOR	A perfect patchwork of old buildings and modern art, with a colourful design

Leuchtende Farben der Provence

Das Le Cloître ist nicht nur zentral, zugleich aber sehr ruhig in Arles gelegen, sondern auch einmalig schön eingerichtet. Die Schweizer Kunstmäzenin Maja Hoffmann, der das Hotel gehört, hat die französisch-libanesische Architektin India Mahdavi mit dem Umbau und der Einrichtung des historischen Gebäudes beauftragt. Bei der Ausstattung wurde nicht gespart, umso mehr verblüffen die Zimmerpreise. Handgenähte Vorhänge aus Leinen und Samt, maßgefertigte Möbel wie Sofas, Schränke und Raumteiler in Kombination mit ausgewählten Möbelstücken der Gebrüder Bouroullec, Gio Ponti sowie aus den Werkstätten von Vittorio Bonacina zieren die sonnendurchfluteten Räume. India Mahdavi selbst hat viele originale Solitäre beigesteuert: Ihr Marmortisch „Bishop" erinnert an eine Schachfigur; das Motiv wiederholt sich in einem Waschtisch aus weiß glasierter Keramik, der schon bei der Morgentoilette für gute Laune sorgt. Das spezielle Licht in Arles hat schon Vincent van Gogh und Paul Gauguin in das Städtchen gelockt, das heute vor allem für das alljährliche Festival der Modernen Fotografie berühmt ist. Die entschiedene Farbgestaltung im Cloître erinnert auf schöne Weise an diese Vermählung von Licht und Schaffenslust. Dazu kommt die Lage des Hauses: Von der Dachterrasse aus schweift der Blick über die Kathedrale Saint Trophime bis zum Antiken Theater. Die vom Schweizer Pharmaunternehmen Hoffmann-La Roche 2014 ins Leben gerufene Fondation Vincent van Gogh liegt nur einen kleinen Spaziergang entfernt. Das Museum fördert die Auseinandersetzung lebender Künstler mit van Goghs Werk. Maja Hoffmann ist die Präsidentin der Stiftung. Auch das etwas außerhalb in der Camargue gelegene Restaurant La Chassagnette gehört ihr. Hier werden sämtliche Gemüse und Kräuter im hauseigenen Biogarten geerntet. Der kleine Ausflug ist ein Muss während eines Aufenthaltes in Arles.

Buchtipp: »Fiesta« von Ernest Hemingway

La Provence aux couleurs éclatantes

Le Cloître à Arles est central, mais aussi très tranquille, et surtout aménagé avec un goût unique. La mécène suisse Maja Hoffmann, propriétaire de l'hôtel, a confié la transformation et l'installation du bâtiment historique à l'architecte franco-libanaise India Mahdavi. Les travaux ont été réalisés sans aucun souci d'épargne, et les prix des chambres en sont d'autant plus étonnants. Des rideaux de lin et velours cousus main, du mobilier sur mesure tel que canapés, armoires et meubles de séparation, associés à d'autres sélectionnés des frères Bouroullec, de Gio Ponti ou des ateliers de Vittorio Bonacina, ornent les pièces baignées de soleil. India Mahdavi elle-même a contribué avec de nombreuses pièces uniques pleines d'originalité : sa table de marbre « Bishop » fait penser à une figure de jeu d'échecs, un motif répété sur une table de toilette en céramique émaillée blanche, garantie de bonne humeur dès la première toilette du matin. La lumière propre à Arles a déjà attiré Vincent van Gogh et Paul Gauguin dans la petite ville, aujourd'hui plus célèbre pour son festival annuel de photographie. Le choix résolu des couleurs du Cloître rappelle en beauté ce mariage de la lumière et du désir créateur. Il faut y ajouter la situation : depuis le toit en terrasse, le regard erre de la cathédrale Saint Trophime au théâtre antique. La Fondation Van Gogh, ouverte en 2014 par le laboratoire pharmaceutique suisse Hoffmann-LaRoche, n'est éloignée que d'une petite promenade. Le musée y favorise la confrontation d'artistes vivants à l'œuvre de van Gogh. Maja Hoffmann est présidente de la fondation. Le restaurant La Chassagnette, un peu à l'écart de la ville, en Camargue, lui appartient lui aussi. Les légumes et les herbes y sont tous cultivés dans le jardin bio. C'est une petite excursion qui s'impose pendant tout séjour à en Arles.

Livre à emporter : « Le soleil se lève aussi » d'Ernest Hemingway

ANREISE	45 min nördlich vom Flughafen Marseille oder 20 min vom Bahnhof oder Flughafen in Avignon. 30 min vom TGV Bahnhof in Nimes
PREIS	€
ZIMMER	19 Zimmer: 11 Doppelzimmer, 2 Einzelzimmer, 1 Superior, 5 Suiten
KÜCHE	Es wird nur Frühstück angeboten, alle Produkte sind lokal und bio. Das Restaurant La Chassagnette 30 min außerhalb von Arles hat einen Michelin-Stern
GESCHICHTE	Teile des Gebäudes stammen aus dem 13. Jahrhundert, neu eröffnet als Hotel 2012
X-FAKTOR	perfektes Patchwork aus alten Gemäuern und moderner Kunst und farbenfrohem Design

ACCÈS	À 45 mn de route au nord de l'aéroport de Marseille et à 20 mn de la gare ou de l'aéroport d'Avignon. À 30 mn de la gare TGV de Nîmes
PRIX	€
CHAMBRES	19 chambres : 11 chambres doubles, 2 chambres simples, 1 superior, 5 suites
RESTAURATION	Petit déjeuner seulement, tous les produits sont issus de l'agriculture biologique locale. Le restaurant La Chassagnette, à 30 mn d'Arles, a une étoile au Michelin
HISTOIRE	Certaines parties du bâtiment datent du XIIIe siècle et ont été réouvertes comme hôtel en 2012
LES « PLUS »	Un mélange parfait de vieux murs, d'art moderne et de design coloré

A Place in the Country...
La Maison Domaine de Bournissac, Provence

La Maison Domaine de Bournissac, Provence

A Place in the Country

This old country inn located in the heart of Provence is just minutes from the town of Saint-Rémy. It is still quite a secret place, even in this much-explored area. At the end of a long gravel road, hidden away, this simple house comes into view. Yet the Domaine de Bournissac has a deceptive exterior; the inside is not quite as simple as it appears to be.

The centuries-old farmhouse has been restored and revived as an oasis of calm. The expert pairing of style and simplicity is unmistakable in these surroundings. Pale colours of marble, stone and bleached wood signal the restful atmosphere to be found within its walls. Every room is different; each one in a muted palette and composed by a sure and artistic hand. Outside, the delightful garden and terrace grant space to sit in the sun and dream, or offer welcome shade cast by a massive old oak tree. In the summer, fields of sunflowers and lavender are in bloom. This is the landscape and light that so inspired Van Gogh, and lures people to it still. However, despite its allusions to the past, traditional farmhouse-style food is decidedly not on the menu. The kitchen has a reputation that has spread a long way from its rural setting.

Book to pack: "Lust for Life: the Story of Vincent van Gogh" by Irving Stone

La Maison Domaine de Bournissac
Montée d'Eyragues
13550 Paluds de Noves
France
Tel: + 33 (0) 490902525
Fax: + 33 (0) 490902526
E-mail: bournissac@wanadoo.fr
Website: www.lamaison-a-bournissac.com

DIRECTIONS	South of Avignon, it is just 5 minutes from Saint-Rémy-de-Provence
RATES	€€
ROOMS	13 rooms
FOOD	Renowned, and drawing on the rich local resources
HISTORY	Part of the building dates back to the 14th century, others are from the 18th century. The Domaine de Bournissac has received guests since 1999
X-FACTOR	A lovely country house in one of the most beautiful parts of France

Ein Platz auf dem Lande

Nur wenige Minuten von Saint-Rémy im Herzen der Provence liegt ein alter Landgasthof. Er ist sogar in dieser touristisch weitgehend erschlossenen Gegend ein Geheimtipp geblieben. Versteckt am Ende eines langen Kieswegs entdeckt man plötzlich ein einfaches Haus. Doch dieser Eindruck täuscht: Die Domaine de Bournissac wirkt nur äußerlich einfach. Das ehemalige, mehrere Jahrhunderte alte Bauernhaus ist heute als Oase der Stille wieder zum Leben erwacht. Stil und Schlichtheit sind eine perfekte Symbiose eingegangen. Die blasse Farbpalette von Marmor, Stein und gebleichtem Holz signalisiert, welch entspannende Atmosphäre innerhalb der Steinmauern zu finden ist. Die Gästezimmer wurden jeweils indiviuell gestaltet, alle jedoch gekonnt und stilsicher und in warmen Farben gehalten. Draußen laden Garten und Terrasse zum Sonnenbaden und Träumen ein, und eine riesige alte Eiche spendet angenehmen Schatten. Im Sommer blühen Sonnenblumen und Lavendel in den Feldern ringsherum. Landschaft und Licht inspirierten einst Van Gogh und ziehen bis heute die Menschen an. Doch etwas überrascht: Trotz der langen Geschichte des Hofs wird hier keine deftige Landhausküche serviert, sondern Gerichte, die die ländlichen Wurzeln längst hinter sich gelassen haben.

Buchtipp: »Vincent van Gogh. Ein Leben in Leidenschaft« von Irving Stone

Dans la campagne provençale

À quelques minutes à peine de Saint-Rémy, en plein coeur de la Provence, se dresse une vieille auberge de campagne. C'est un endroit encore secret dans cette région qui n'en compte plus guère. Tout au bout d'une longue route de gravier surgit une maison toute simple. Mais que l'on ne s'y trompe pas : l'intérieur est beaucoup moins modeste qu'il n'y paraît. Cette ancienne ferme séculaire a été restaurée, transformée en une oasis de tranquillité, où raffinement et simplicité vont de pair. Les teintes discrètes du marbre, de la pierre et du bois brut annoncent l'atmosphère paisible qui règne entre ses murs. Chaque chambre est différente des autres, mais toutes sont dotées de couleurs douces et décorées avec beaucoup de goût. À l'extérieur, le jardin et la terrasse se prêtent au repos et à la rêverie, à l'ombre d'un imposant chêne centenaire. En été, les champs de tournesol et de lavande déploient leurs symphonies de couleurs. C'est le paysage et la lumière qui ont inspiré Van Gogh, et qui continuent d'attirer les visiteurs. En dépit de son passé rural, l'auberge ne sert pas de plats campagnards : l'excellente cuisine a depuis longtemps oublié ses origines champêtres.

Livre à emporter : « La Vie passionnée de Vincent van Gogh » de Irving Stone

ANREISE	Südlich von Avignon und 5 Minuten von Saint-Rémy-de-Provence entfernt
PREIS	€€
ZIMMER	13 Zimmer
KÜCHE	Renommierte Küche, die sich am kulinarischen Reichtum der Region orientiert
GESCHICHTE	Teile des Gebäudes stammen aus dem 14. Jahrhundert, andere aus dem 18. Jahrhundert. Die Domaine de Bournissac ist seit 1999 Hotel
X-FAKTOR	Ein wunderschönes Landhaus in einem wunderschönen Teil Frankreichs

ACCÈS	Au sud d'Avignon, à 5 minutes de Saint-Rémy-de-Provence
PRIX	€€
CHAMBRES	13 chambres
RESTAURATION	Réputée, tire profit des ressources locales
HISTOIRE	Quelques parties du bâtiment sont du XIVe siècle, les autres du XVIIIe siècle ; le Domaine de Bournissac est un hôtel depuis 1999
LES « PLUS »	Une ravissante maison de campagne dans une région non moins superbe

A Poetic Hideaway...
Villa Fiordaliso, Lago di Garda

Villa Fiordaliso, Lago di Garda

A Poetic Hideaway

The romance of times gone by is almost palpable in the air here. The view across the lake is much the same as it was back when the poet Gabriele D'Annunzio looked out from his window. Perhaps he had writer's block and was hoping to be inspired as he gazed at the tranquil waters.

Villa Fiordaliso is an ideal place to hide away, whether or not you are prone to poetry or prose – the setting is poetic in itself. Framed by cypresses, pines and olive trees at the edge of Lake Garda, the elegant old villa has a sense of absolute calm. No doubt, if the walls of the classic interior could speak, many anecdotes might be told of those who have stayed here, from poets to dictators. For utter romantics, there is a most enticing place close by; the city of Verona, famed for being the source of the tragic love story of Romeo and Juliet. Walking through the streets and underneath the balconies of the "pair of star-crossed lovers", you believe the tale to be true.

You will very likely become lyrical over the cuisine, since the menu may not have been written by a poet, but is certainly cooked by artists. Parting from Villa Fiordaliso will indeed be an occasion for "sweet sorrow".

Books to pack: "Romeo and Juliet" by William Shakespeare
"The Flame" by Gabriele D'Annunzio

Villa Fiordaliso	
Via Zanardelli 150	
25083 Gardone Riviera	
Italy	
Tel: + 39 (0) 365 201 58	
Fax: + 39 (0) 365 290 011	
E-mail: info@villafiordaliso.it	
Website: www.villafiordaliso.it	

DIRECTIONS	40 km/25 m north-west of Verona
RATES	€€€
ROOMS	5 rooms
FOOD	A Michelin-starred restaurant
X-FACTOR	Utterly romantic

Ein malerisches Versteck

An diesem Ort spürt man den Zauber vergangener Zeiten.
Der Blick über den See ist noch derselbe wie damals, als der
Dichter Gabriele D'Annunzio aus seinem Fenster schaute.
Vielleicht hatte er einen Schreibblock dabei und ließ sich
von dem ruhigen Gewässer vor seinen Augen inspirieren.
Die Villa Fiordaliso ist ein idealer Ort, um sich zurückzuziehen.
Allein die Landschaft ist reinste Poesie! In der von Zypres-
sen, Pinien und Olivenbäumen eingerahmten alten Villa am
Ufer des Gardasees herrscht absolute Stille. Wenn die Wände
des klassischen Interieurs reden könnten, wür-den sie zwei-
fellos hübsche kleine Anekdoten über die vielen berühmten
Persönlichkeiten – ob Dichter oder Diktatoren – erzählen,
die hier genächtigt haben. Romantiker finden ganz in der
Nähe einen besonders reizvollen Ort, nämlich die Stadt
Verona, die durch die tragische Liebesgeschichte von Romeo
und Julia weltberühmt wurde. Wenn man durch die Straßen
und unter den Balkonen entlangpromeniert, könnte man fast
glauben, die Geschichte habe sich wirklich zugetragen.
Die Küche der Villa Fiordaliso ist ein wahres Gedicht, und
auch wenn die Speisekarte vielleicht nicht von Dichterhand
geschrieben wurde, sind es doch Künstler, die hier wirken.
Buchtipps: »Romeo und Julia« von William Shakespeare
»Das Feuer« von Gabriele D'Annunzio

Un refuge romantique

Il flotte ici un air de nostalgie romantique. La vue sur le lac
est sûrement très semblable à celle dont jouissait le poète
Gabriele D'Annunzio depuis sa fenêtre. Devant une page
blanche, peut-être recherchait-il l'inspiration en contemplant
ces eaux paisibles …
La Villa Fiordaliso est un refuge idéal, même pour ceux qui
ne taquinent pas la plume. Le cadre est un poème à lui seul :
cernée de cyprès, de pins et d'oliviers, solitaire sur une rive
du lac de Garde, l'élégante villa ancienne respire le calme
absolu. Si les murs de l'édifice néoclassique pouvaient parler,
ils ne tariraient pas d'anecdotes sur ses résidents – des
poètes aux dictateurs. Pour les esprits romantiques, la ville
de Vérone, théâtre des tragiques amours de Roméo et
Juliette, se trouve à proximité. Une promenade dans les
ruelles et sous les balcons vous fera peut-être croire à l'histoire des malheureux amants.
Mais réservez plutôt votre lyrisme pour la table : si la carte
n'a pas été rédigée par un poète, les mets sont certainement
cuisinés par de véritables artistes.
Livres à emporter : « Le Feu » de Gabriele D'Annunzio
« Roméo et Juliette » de William Shakespeare

ANREISE	40 km nordwestlich von Verona
PREIS	€€€
ZIMMER	5 Zimmer
KÜCHE	Ein mit mehreren Michelin-Sternen ausgezeichnetes Restaurant
X-FAKTOR	Romantik pur

ACCÈS	À 40 km au nord-est de Vérone
PRIX	€€€
CHAMBRES	5 chambres
RESTAURATION	Plusieurs étoiles au Michelin
LES « PLUS »	Le summum du romantisme

A World Afloat...
Belmond Hotel Cipriani, Venezia

Belmond Hotel Cipriani, Venezia

A World Afloat

"Streets flooded. Please advise." So said a telegram once sent from here by a humorous writer. But seriously, there is not much that can match the first sight of Venice. You should choose to arrive by boat; the ride along the Grand Canal, past palaces and churches, then turning into the lagoon of San Marco to see the sunlight glinting on the domes of the Doge's Palace, is a memorable one. The boat will bring you to Palazzo Vendramin, the 15th-century residence on one of the many islands that make up this ancient city. The Palazzo's beautiful arched windows frame one of the most romantic and famous views in the world: the front-row view of St. Mark's Square. With only a few suites, it is more akin to an elegant private home; however, it is part of the famed Belmond Hotel Cipriani, but a short stroll away, across the courtyard. And guests may share in all of the Cipriani's wealth of resources. Just a few minutes from its calm cloisters is a busier, noisier place. This special city of the past is quite like a magnet. Yet, off the main sightseeing trail, there is a quieter, slower Venice still to be glimpsed.

Books to pack: "Death In Venice" by Thomas Mann
"A Venetian Reckoning" by Donna Leon

Belmond Hotel Cipriani
Isola della Giudecca, 10
30133 Venezia
Italy
Tel: +39 (0) 41 240 801
Fax: +39 (0) 41 5207745
E-mail: info.cip@belmond.com
Website: www.belmond.com/hotelcipriani

DIRECTIONS	30 minutes by boat from Marco Polo airport
RATES	€€€€
ROOMS	16 rooms and suites at the Palazzo Vendramin and the Palazzetto, 82 rooms and suites at the Hotel Cipriani
FOOD	The cooking at the Cipriani and Cip's Club is to die for. In the Oro Restaurant, Michelin star-winning chef Davide Bisetto serves up his imaginative creations
HISTORY	The Palazzo Vendramin was built in the 15th century. It opened as a hotel in 1991, and the Palazzetto Nani Barbaro in 1998
X-FACTOR	One of the most incomparable places in the world

Eine Welt im Fluss

»Alle Straßen unter Wasser. Was ist zu tun?«, lautete das Telegramm, das ein Schriftsteller mit Humor hier einst aufgab. Doch im Ernst: Der erste Anblick von Venedig lässt sich mit nichts vergleichen.

Wenn es geht, sollte man in der Stadt mit dem Boot ankommen. Die Fahrt auf dem Canal Grande vorbei an Palazzi und Kirchen, der Blick in die Lagune von San Marco, wenn die Sonne über den Dogenpalast dahingleitet, ist unvergesslich. Mit dem Boot gelangen Sie auch zum Palazzo Vendramin, einem Anwesen aus dem 15. Jahrhundert, das auf einer der vielen Inseln Venedigs liegt. Von hier aus bietet sich – gerahmt durch die Bogenfenster des Palazzo – ein fantastischer Blick auf den Markusplatz – einer der schönsten, berühmtesten und romantischsten Ausblicke der Welt. Der Palazzo erinnert mit seinen wenigen Suiten eher an ein elegantes Privathaus als an ein Hotel. Doch ist er Teil des berühmten Belmond Hotel Cipriani, das sich in einem wenige Minuten dauernden Spaziergang quer über einen Innenhof erreichen lässt. Den Gästen des Palazzo stehen die vielfältigen Angebote des Cipriani ebenfalls zur Verfügung. Nur wenige Minuten von der fast klösterlichen Ruhe und Beschaulichkeit entfernt, können sie in ein bunteres und lauteres Leben eintauchen.

Venedig scheint eine Stadt aus der Vergangenheit zu sein, doch ihre Anziehungskraft ist bis heute ungebrochen. Wie schön, dass es neben den typischen Touristenattraktionen noch ein leiseres und ruhigeres Venedig zu entdecken gibt.

Buchtipps: »Der Tod in Venedig« von Thomas Mann
»Venezianische Scharade« von Donna Leon

Entre terre et eau

«Rues inondées. Que faire?». Tel est le message télégraphique qu'envoya un visiteur de Venise qui ne manquait pas d'humour! Trêve de plaisanteries ; rien ou presque n'égale l'impact de la première vision de Venise.

Arrivez de préférence à Venise par bateau. Le trajet le long du Grand Canal et de ses palais et églises, puis l'entrée dans la lagune de Saint-Marc pour voir le soleil scintiller sur les toits du Palais des Doges, est tout à fait mémorable. Le bateau vous amènera au Palazzo Vendramin. Cette résidence du XVe siècle se dresse sur l'une des nombreuses îles qui forment la ville ancienne. Le Palazzo donne sur la place Saint-Marc ; ses superbes fenêtres en plein cintre encadrent l'une des places les plus romantiques et célèbres du monde. N'abritant que quelques suites, il évoque une élégante résidence privée, bien qu'il fasse partie de l'illustre Belmond hôtel Cipriani, situé seulement à quelques pas, de l'autre côté de la cour. Ses hôtes peuvent profiter de tout ce que le Cipriani a à offrir. À quelques minutes à peine de la tranquillité de ses murs, s'étend une place bruyante et fort animée.

Cette ville d'un autre temps est en effet un véritable aimant touristique. Néanmoins, au-delà des sentiers battus, se cache une Venise plus nonchalante et sereine .

Livres à emporter : « La Mort à Venise » de Thomas Mann
« Un Vénitien anonyme » de Donna Leon

ANREISE	30 Minuten Anfahrt mit dem Boot vom Marco Polo Flughafen
PREIS	€€€€
ZIMMER	16 Zimmer und Suiten im Palazzo Vendramin und im Palazzetto, 82 Zimmer und Suiten im Hotel Cipriani
KÜCHE	Für die Küche des Cipriani und des Cip's Club kann man schon freiwillig zum Schiffbrüchigen werden. Im Oro Restaurant serviert der Michelinstern gekrönte Chef Davide Bisetto seine fantasievollen Kreationen
GESCHICHTE	Der Palazzo Vendramin wurde im 15. Jahrhundert erbaut. Er öffnete als Hotel im Jahr 1991, der Palazzetto Nani Barbaro 1998
X-FAKTOR	Einer der unvergleichlichsten Orte der Welt

ACCÈS	À 30 minutes de bateau de l'aéroport Marco Polo
PRIX	€€€€
CHAMBRES	16 chambres et suites dans le Palazzo Vendramin et le Palazzetto, 82 chambres et suites à l'hôtel Cipriani
RESTAURATION	On se ferait naufragé volontaire pour la cuisine du Cipriani et du Cip's Club. Au restaurant Oro, le chef étoilé au Michelin Davide Bisetto sert ses créations pleines de fantaisie
HISTOIRE	Le Palazzo Vendramin a été construit au XVe siècle. Il a ouvert sous forme d'hôtel en 1991, le Palazzetto Nani Barbaro en 1998
LES « PLUS »	L'un des lieux les plus inoubliables du monde

In a Blue Mood...
Hotel Parco dei Principi, Sorrento

Hotel Parco dei Principi, Sorrento

In a Blue Mood

According to the legend, the mermaids who tempted Ulysses with their enchanting songs lived in the Sorrentine Sea.

In the real world, the charms of the Hotel Parco dei Principi has lured other travellers to that same coastline. Built on a cliff in one of the most famous gardens in Italy, the hotel's clean lines and cool blue and white decor seem to reflect the colour of the sea below. Master architect Gio Ponti created the hotel in the 1960s, applying his one-colour theory of interior design to striking effect, from the tiled floors to the window blinds. The spacious terraces offer a dazzling view of the blue Bay of Naples and the volcano of Mount Vesuvius. An elevator or stairway built into an ancient cave takes the guests down to the hotel's private jetty and beach. Or bathers may prefer the swimming pool, secluded in the historic park that was once the property of various noble families.

Nearby is the picturesque town of Sorrento that crowns the rocky cliffs close to the end of the peninsula. In the cafés you can taste delicious cakes, ice cream, and a glass of "Limoncello", the local lemon liqueur, just some of the many attractions of this much-celebrated place.

Books to pack: "The Island of the Day Before" by Umberto Eco "Thus Spoke Bellavista: Naples, Love and Liberty" by Luciano De Crescenzo

Hotel Parco dei Principi
Via Rota 44
80067 Sorrento
Italy
Tel: + 39 (0) 81 878 46 44
Fax: + 39 (0) 81 878 37 86
E-mail: info@grandhotelparcodeiprincipi.it
Website: www.royalgroup.it/parcodeiprincipi

DIRECTIONS	On the outskirts of Sorrento, 48 km/30 m south from Naples
RATES	€€
ROOMS	96 rooms, open all year round; ask for a room with sea view
FOOD	Neapolitan cuisine and local specialties in a beautiful restaurant
HISTORY	Built and opened in 1962
X-FACTOR	Enduring style in a stunning location

Blaue Stunde

Der Legende zufolge war es vor Sorrent, wo Odysseus und seine Gefährten von den Gesängen der Sirenen betört wurden. In der realen Welt werden indes andere Reisende vom Zauber des Hotels Parco dei Principi an diese Küste gelockt. Die klaren Linien und das kühle Blau und Weiß dieses auf einer Steilküste aus Tuffstein erbauten Hotels, welches inmitten eines der berühmtesten Gärten Italiens liegt, scheinen das Farbenspiel des Meeres widerzuspie-geln. Der Meisterarchitekt Gio Ponti, der das Hotel in den 1960er-Jahren entwarf, hat hier seine Philosophie von einer monochromen Innenraumgestaltung mit spektakulärem Erfolg umgesetzt: von den gekachelten Fußböden bis hin zu den Jalousien.

Die großzügigen Terrassen bieten fantastische Ausblicke auf die blaue Bucht von Neapel und den Vesuv. Über einen Aufzug oder eine Treppe, die durch das Innere des Tuffsteins führt, gelangen Gäste zu dem Privatstrand des Hotels, der auch über einen eigenen Steg verfügt. Wassernixen können sich natürlich auch im Pool tummeln. Dieser liegt versteckt in dem historischen Park, der sich früher im Besitz verschiedener Adelsfamilien befand.

In der Nähe liegt die malerische Stadt Sorrent auf den Felsklippen am Ende der Halbinsel. Hier können Sie sich in den Cafés an köstlichem Kuchen, Eis-Spezialitäten und einem Glas Limoncello, dem in der Region produzierten Zitronenlikör, erbauen, um dann eine der zahlreichen Sehenswürdigkeiten dieses viel gepriesenen Ortes zu erkunden.

Buchtipps: »Die Insel des vorigen Tages« von Umberto Eco »Also sprach Bellavista. Neapel, Liebe und Freiheit« von Luciano De Crescenzo

Conte bleu

Selon la légende, les sirènes qui séduisirent Ulysse et ses compagnons par leur chant trompeur vivaient dans la mer de Sorrente.

Dans le monde réel, les charmes de l'Hôtel Parco dei Principi ont attiré d'autres voyageurs vers ce littoral. Les lignes pures et le décor bleu et blanc de l'hôtel, construit sur une falaise dans l'un des jardins les plus célèbres d'Italie, semblent refléter les couleurs de la mer qui danse à ses pieds. Du carrelage aux stores, le célèbre architecte Gio Ponti, qui a créé l'hôtel dans les années 1960, a appliqué avec bonheur sa théorie selon laquelle la décoration d'intérieur se doit d'être monochrome.

Depuis les terrasses spacieuses, on découvre une vue éblouissante sur la mer bleue de la baie de Naples et sur le Vésuve. Les clients de l'hôtel descendent à la jetée et à la plage privées par un ascenseur ou un escalier qui traverse une grotte ancienne. On peut aussi se baigner dans la piscine, cachée dans le parc historique qui a appartenu autrefois à diverses familles nobles.

Tout près, la ville pittoresque de Sorrente couronne les falaises rocheuses proches de l'extrémité de la péninsule. Dans les salons de thé, on peut goûter aux gâteaux délicieux, aux glaces ou au limoncello, la liqueur de citron locale, quelques-uns seulement des nombreux attraits de cet endroit si célèbre.

Livres à emporter: « L'Ile du jour d'avant » d'Umberto Eco « Ainsi parlait Bellavista » de Luciano De Crescenzo

ANREISE	Am Stadtrand von Sorrent, 48 km südlich von Neapel
PREIS	€€
ZIMMER	96 Zimmer, ganzjährig geöffnet; fragen Sie nach einem Zimmer mit Meerblick
KÜCHE	Neapolitanische Küche und lokale Spezialitäten in einem wunderschönen, eleganten Restaurant
GESCHICHTE	Erbaut und geöffnet 1962
X-FAKTOR	Zeitloser Stil in atemberaubender Umgebung

ACCÈS	Dans les environs de Sorrente, à 48 km au sud de Naple
PRIX	€€
CHAMBRES	96 chambres, ouvertes toute l'année ; demandez une chambre avec vue sur la mer
RESTAURATION	Cuisine napolitaine et spécialités locales servies dans un restaurant splendide
HISTOIRE	Construit et ouvert en 1962
LES « PLUS »	Style intemporel, dans un cadre éblouissant

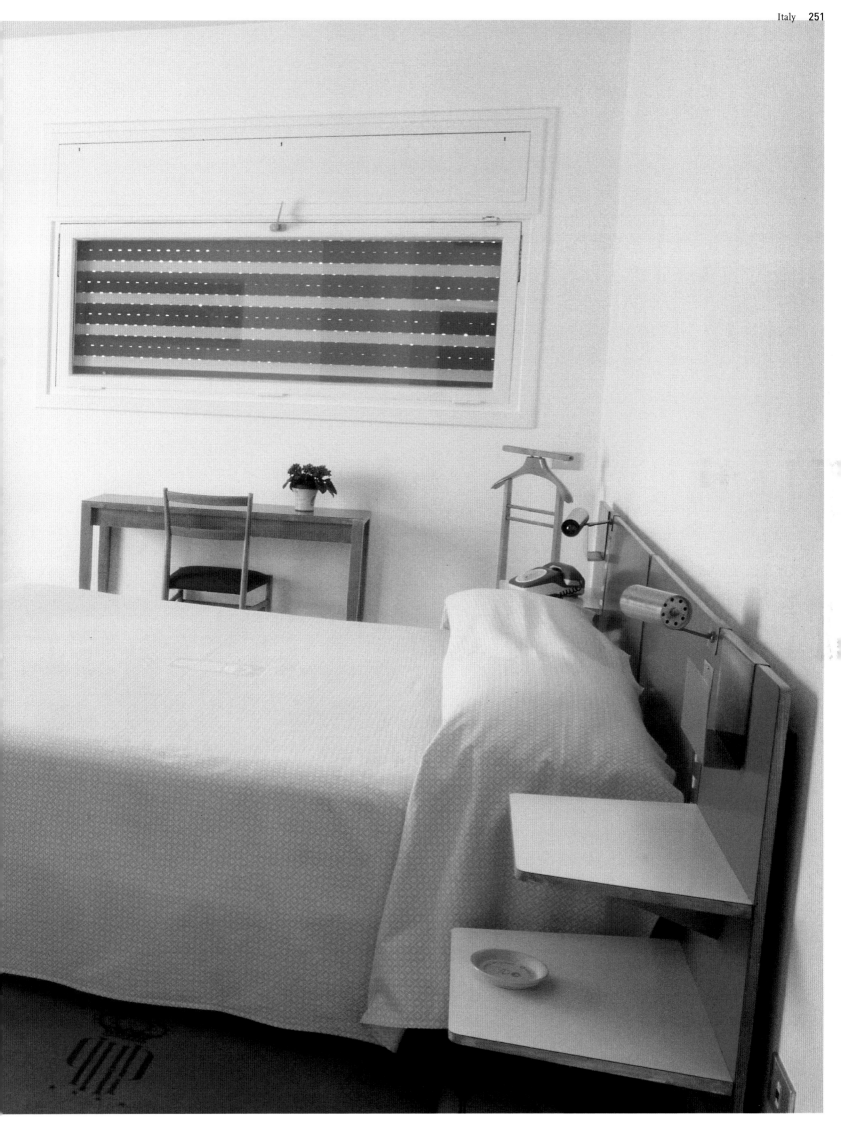

Changing Rooms...
L'Atelier sul Mare, Sicilia

L' Atelier sul Mare, Sicilia

Changing Rooms

As a matter of course, guests of this hotel will want to stay each night in a different room than the one before. At L'Atelier sul Mare, it is common to change rooms daily, so that the guest may experience all that this unique hotel has to offer. Just a few steps from the sea in one of Sicily's most beautiful bays, on the coast between Palermo and Messina, the hotel has a rare concept: a place where the rooms double up as exhibition pieces. Well-known artists have created many of the rooms. The interiors that have sprung from their fertile imaginations are quite fantastic and dramatic spaces, all with poetic names. "Dreams amongst the Drawings" is themed around the growth of writing, "The Prophet's Room" pays homage to film director Pasolini, and in "The Tower of Sigismondo", a circular tower descends from the transparent ceiling, while at its base, an enormous round bed rotates slowly. This might seem more like a museum than a hotel, except for the fact that, as its creator explains, "only when a visitor enters and lives in a room will the work of art be fully realized; the use of the room is an integral and fundamental part of the work."

**Books to pack: "The Leopard" by Giuseppe Tomasi di Lampedusa
"The Lives of the Artists" by Giorgio Vasari**

L'Atelier sul Mare	
Via Cesare Battisti, 4	
98079 Castel di Tusa (Messina)	
Sicily	
Italy	
Tel: + 39 (0) 921 334295	
Fax: + 39 (0) 921 334283	
E-mail: antoniopresti@	
fondazionefiumaradarte.org	
Website: www.ateliersulmare.com	

DIRECTIONS	2 hours' drive west from Palermo, near the town of Cefalù
RATES	€
ROOMS	40 rooms and suites; 24 standard rooms decorated by young European artists, 14 rooms created by contemporary artists
FOOD	Traditional Sicilian fare, artfully served
HISTORY	Built in the 1975 as a hotel, the Atelier Sul Mare was transformed in 1991
X-FACTOR	Being the living part of an artwork

Tapetenwechsel

Wenn Sie hier Gast sind, werden Sie sicher jede Nacht in einem anderen Zimmer verbringen wollen. Der tägliche Tapetenwechsel gehört im L'Atelier sul Mare zum guten Ton, denn die Gäste sollen so viel wie möglich von ihrem Aufenthalt in diesem einzigartigen Hotel profitieren können.

Nur wenige Schritte vom Meer entfernt in einer der schönsten Buchten Siziliens an der Küste zwischen Palermo und Messina gelegen, verwirklicht dieses Hotel ein außergewöhnliches Konzept, bei dem die Gästezimmer gleichzeitig Ausstellungsräume sind. Viele Räume wurden von bekannten Künstlern gestaltet und tragen entsprechend der fantasievollen Interieurs poetische Namen: »Träume inmitten der Zeichnungen« hat die Entwicklung des Schreibens zum Thema, »Der Raum des Propheten« ist eine visuelle Hommage an den Regisseur Pier Paolo Pasolini und im »Turm von Sigismondo« hängt von der durchsichtigen Decke ein runder Turm herab, – darunter dreht sich ein riesiges Bett langsam im Kreise.

Dieses Haus wirkt eher wie ein Museum als wie ein Hotel, doch sein Gründer erklärt, dass »das Kunstwerk erst dann vollendet ist, wenn ein Besucher sich mit dem Raum auseinandersetzt und darin lebt. Die Nutzung der Räume ist integraler, ja unabdingbarer Aspekt der Werke.«

Buchtipps: »Der Leopard« von Giuseppe Tomasi di Lampedusa
»Pier Paolo Pasolini. Eine Biografie« von Nico Naldini

De chambre en chambre

À coup sûr, les clients de l'Atelier sul Mare voudront changer de chambre toutes les nuits ! Ici, les hôtes ont coutume de déménager chaque jour pour profiter au maximum de cet hôtel hors du commun. Situé entre Palerme et Messine, dans l'une des plus belles baies siciliennes et à seulement quelques pas de la mer, l'hôtel concrétise un concept inédit selon lequel chaque chambre est un objet d'art en soi. La plupart d'entre elles ont été créées par des artistes connus et sont dotées de noms poétiques à l'image de ces intérieurs originaux: celle des « Rêves parmi les dessins » s'inspire de l'évolution de l'écriture, « La Chambre du prophète » rend hommage au metteur en scène Pier Paolo Pasolini et dans « La tour de Sigismondo » une tour circulaire descend du plafond transparent. À son pied, un immense lit circulaire tourne lentement sur lui-même. On pourrait se croire dans un musée plutôt que dans un hôtel, mais comme l'explique son créateur, « l'œuvre d'art n'est complète que lorsqu'un hôte a pénétré dans la chambre et y vit ; l'utilisation de la chambre forme une partie intégrante et fondamentale de l'œuvre. »

Livres à emporter: « Le Guépard » de Giuseppe Tomasi di Lampedusa
« Pier Paolo Pasolini : Biographie » de Nico Naldini

ANREISE	2 Fahrstunden westlich von Palermo, in der Nähe von Cefalù
PREIS	€
ZIMMER	40 Zimmer und Suiten; 24 von jungen europäischen Künstlern gestaltete Standardzimmer, 14 von zeitgenössischen Künstlern gestaltete Zimmer
KÜCHE	Traditionelle sizilianische Gerichte, kunstvoll präsentiert
GESCHICHTE	1975 errichtet und 1991 umgebaut
X-FAKTOR	Hier sind Sie lebender Bestandteil eines Kunstwerks

ACCÈS	À deux heures de route de Palerme, près de la ville de Cefalù
PRIX	€
CHAMBRES	40 chambres et suites ; 24 chambres standard, décorées par de jeunes artistes européens, 14 créées par des artistes contemporains
RESTAURATION	Cuisine sicilienne traditionnelle, servie avec art
HISTOIRE	Hôtel construit en 1975 et transformé en 1991
LES « PLUS »	Devenir l'élément vivant d'une œuvre d'art

In the Shade of Fig Trees...
Casa Talía, Sicilia

Casa Talía, Sicilia

In the Shade of Fig Trees
Surrounded by breathtakingly beautiful Baroque façades, the town of Modica has been declared a UNESCO World Heritage site, but even with this recognition there are still gems waiting to be discovered. On a hill between small gardens and olive and fig trees there are cottages that have been carefully restored with traditional Sicilian craftsmanship and now serve as guest rooms. Each of the 11 rooms has been individually decorated with old tiles, traditional bamboo ceilings, and terra-cotta floors. Furnished mainly with Sicilian antiques, nevertheless the rooms appear uncomplicated, and therefore seem modern. Here is the perfect place, then, to read a book in the shade of a fig tree – Slow Living at its essence. In between naps and before dusk and dinner you can stroll down the streets into the picturesque centre of Modica and find something nice to do. Especially recommended is the Caffè dell'Arte: enjoy a mandorla granita, a delicious ice cream made to the café's own recipe, or lounge on the chairs in front of the house as you sip the unique Caffè Shakerato (cold espresso, shaken on ice with a dash of sugar). Right next door is the best chocolate factory in Sicily, the Antica Dolceria Bonajuto, which also produces other delicious Sicilian sweets that you can have wrapped up to take away and relish in the hotel garden.
Book to pack: "The Godfather" by Mario Puzo

Casa Talía
Via Exaudinos, 1/9
Modica (RG) Italy
Tel: +39 (0) 932 752075
Mobile: + 39 (0) 335 5486656
E-mail: info@casatalia.it
www.casatalia.it
Open all year around

DIRECTIONS	2 hours' drive southeast from Catania airport. There is a direct bus line from the airport
RATES	€€
ROOMS	11 rooms, each with its own small garden or terrace
FOOD	Only breakfast in the garden, with fresh juices and pastries and stunning views of the baroque façades of Modica. Some restaurants and cafes are within walking distance
HISTORY	The Milanese architects Marco Giunta and Viviana Haddad bought the property in 2002 and opened it in 2005 with three rooms. If enough money is saved, additional rooms are restored and so new premises are added every year
X-FACTOR	Casa Talia rests on the concept of Slow Living: it is not an empty promise, but one that is lovingly fulfilled

Im Schatten von Feigenbäumen

Das Städtchen Modica wurde von der UNESCO zu einem Bestandteil des Weltkulturerbes erklärt, und selbst hier, umgeben von atemberaubend schönen, barocken Fassaden, gibt es noch immer ein Kleinod zu entdecken. Auf einer Anhöhe zwischen kleinen Gärten und Oliven- und Feigenbäumen stehen dort kleine Häuschen, die mit traditionell sizilianischer Handwerkskunst behutsam restauriert wurden und mittlerweile als Gästezimmer dienen. Ein jedes der insgesamt 11 Zimmer wurde individuell eingerichtet – mit alten Fliesen, traditionellen Bambusdecken, Terrakottaböden. Möbliert vor allem mit sizilianischen Antiquitäten, aber dennoch wirken die Räume sehr schlicht und dadurch modern. Ein perfekter Ort also, um im Schatten eines Feigenbaumes ein Buch zu lesen – Slow Living eben. Zwischendurch ein Nickerchen und vor dem Abend(b)rot die Gässchen hinabsteigen, um sich im malerischen Zentrum Modicas etwas Gutes zu tun. Dort ist vor allem das Caffè dell'Arte zu empfehlen: ein Granita Mandorla, köstliches Eis nach Hausrezept, oder schlürfen Sie auf den Stühlen vor dem Haus den einmaligen Caffè Shakerato (kalten, auf Eis geschüttelten Espresso mit einer Prise Zucker). Gleich nebenan befindet sich die beste Schokoladenmanufaktur Siziliens, die Antica Dolceria Bonajuto, die auch andere köstliche sizilianische Süßigkeiten herstellt, die man sich verpacken lässt, um sie genüsslich im Hotelgarten durchzuprobieren.

Buchtipp: »Die Unvorhersehbarkeit der Liebe« von Goliarda Sapienza

À l'ombre des figuiers

La petite ville de Modica a été inscrite par l'UNESCO au patrimoine culturel mondial et même ici, entouré de façades baroques d'une beauté époustouflante, il reste toujours un trésor à découvrir. Sur une hauteur, entre de petits jardins, des oliviers et des figuiers, de petites maisons ont été soigneusement restaurées par l'artisanat d'art sicilien traditionnel et abritent aujourd'hui des chambres d'hôtes. Les 11 chambres sont toutes aménagées différemment à grand renfort de carrelages anciens, toits de bambou traditionnels ou sols en terre cuite. Meublées pour l'essentiel d'antiquités siciliennes, elles sont cependant très simples, ce qui leur confère une certaine modernité. L'endroit est parfait pour lire à l'ombre d'un figuier — c'est le Slow Living. Avec de temps en temps un petit somme et avant le repas froid du crépuscule, une descente par les ruelles du centre pittoresque de Modica pour se faire plaisir. Le Caffè dell'Arte en particulier ne saurait être trop recommandé : son Granita Mandorla, ses savoureuses recettes maison de glace ou le Caffè Shakerato sans égal (expresso froid versé sur des glaçons avec une pincée de sucre) à siroter sur les chaises devant la maison. Juste à côté, la meilleure manufacture de chocolat de Sicile, l'Antica Dolceria Bonajuto, produit aussi de délicieuses sucreries siciliennes à emporter pour s'en délecter dans le jardin de l'hôtel.

Livre à emporter : « L'Art de la joie » de Goliarda Sapienza

ANREISE	2 Std. Fahrt südöstlich vom Flughafen Catania. Es gibt eine direkte Buslinie vom Flughafen	ACCÈS	2 heures de route au sud-est de l'aéroport de Catane. Bus direct depuis l'aéroport
PREIS	€€	PRIX	€€
ZIMMER	11 Zimmer, alle mit eigenem kl. Garten oder Terrasse	CHAMBRES	11 chambres, toutes avec un petit jardin ou une terrasse
KÜCHE	Frühstück im Garten mit frischen Säften und Gebäck und herrlichem Blick auf Modica. Einige Restaurants und Cafés befinden sich in Fußnähe	RESTAURATION	Petit déjeuner, dans le jardin, avec jus de fruits frais et pâtisseries et la magnifique vue sur Modica. Quelques restaurants et cafés sont accessibles à pied
GESCHICHTE	Das Mailänder Architektenpaar Marco Guinta und Viviana Haddad kaufte das Grundstück 2002 und eröffnete 2005 mit drei Zimmern. Wenn genug Geld gespart ist, werden weitere Räume restauriert	HISTOIRE	Les architectes milanais Marco Guinta et Viviana Haddad ont acheté le terrain en 2002 et ont ouvert en 2005 avec trois chambres. Dès qu'ils ont assez d'économies, ils en restaurent de nouvelles
X-FAKTOR	Das Slow-Living-Konzept hinter Casa Talia ist keine leere Versprechung, sondern mit Liebe betriebene Wirklichkeit	LES « PLUS »	Le concept de Slow Living n'est pas une promesse en l'air, mais une réalité cultivée avec amour

Style Beacon...
Portixol Hotel y Restaurante, Mallorca

Portixol Hotel y Restaurante, Mallorca

Style Beacon

Cool Swedish style transposed to a warm Mediterranean climate seems a near-perfect union. This pairing has given rise to the Portixol Hotel y Restaurante. Designed and built in 1956 by a Spanish architect, the Portixol was rescued from years of neglect and revitalized by its Swedish proprietors, who describe the hotel's style as "marine art deco". The white low-rise structure stands out against the deep blue Majorcan sky, like a cubed lighthouse watching over the harbour. Inside, it is a serene blend of Scandinavian and Spanish modernism. Some of the original 1950s furniture and fittings have been restored, but most of the interior is newly designed, complementing the classic clean lines of the architecture. The hotel's generously sized swimming pool and the sun lounges alongside it are original, re-established as a glamorous lounging place for guests.

Although one of this holiday island's many beaches is just a few metres from the hotel, and the atmospheric old town of Palma is only a short walk away, it would be understandable if visitors to the Portixol chose to stay within its elegant walls.

Books to pack: "A Winter in Majorca" by George Sand
"Tamara de Lempicka: A Life of Deco and Decadence" by Laura Claridge

Portixol Hotel y Restaurante
Calle Sirena 27
07006 Palma de Mallorca
Spain
Tel: + 34 971 27 18 00
Fax: + 34 971 27 50 25
E-mail: hotel@portixol.com
Website: www.portixol.com

DIRECTIONS	1.5 km/1 m from Palma de Mallorca
RATES	€
ROOMS	25 rooms, including suites
FOOD	This restaurant is especially renowned for its modern Mediterranean cuisine
HISTORY	Built and opened in 1956, modernized in 1999
X-FACTOR	Style and sun

Das kommt mir schwedisch vor

Kühler schwedischer Stil in warmem, mediterranem Klima –
eine traumhafte Kombination, die Sie im Hotel Portixol
verwirklicht finden. Dieses 1956 von einem spanischen
Architekten entworfene Hotel wurde von den jetzigen schwedischen Besitzern vor dem Verfall gerettet und renoviert.
Den Stil des Portixol bezeichnen die neuen Hausherren als
»maritimes Art déco«. Das flache, weiße Gebäude, das sich
gegen den tiefblauen Himmel über Mallorca abhebt, wacht
wie ein kubischer Leuchtturm über den Hafen. Das Innere
des Hauses besticht durch eine heitere Mischung aus skandi-
navischem und spanischem Modernismus. Einige der Origi-
nalmöbel und -einrichtungen aus den 1950er-Jahren hat man
restaurieren lassen, aber der Großteil der Interieurs wurde
in Abstimmung auf die klassischen, klaren Linien der Architektur neu entworfen. Der großzügige Pool des Hotels und
die zugehörigen Sonnenliegen wurden als stilvolle Oase,
in der sich Gäste des Hauses entspannen können, original
erhalten.
Obwohl das Haus nur wenige Meter von einem der zahlreichen Strände der Ferieninsel und gerade einmal zwei Kilo-
meter von der stimmungsvollen Altstadt von Palma entfernt
liegt, ist es nur zu verständlich, wenn Besucher die eleganten
Räume des Hotel Portixol vorziehen sollten.
**Buchtipps: »Ein Winter auf Mallorca« von George Sand
»Tamara de Lempicka. Ein Leben für Dekor und Dekadenz« von
Laura Claridge**

Une touche suédoise dans un décor méditerranéen

Dans une combinaison proche de la perfection, l'hôtel
Portixol associe l'élégance discrète du style suédois et la chaleur méditerranéenne. Dessiné et construit en 1956 par un
architecte espagnol, puis laissé à l'abandon durant de longues années, le Portixol a été repris en main par ses propriétaires suédois qui qualifient son style « d'Art Déco marin ».
Sa basse silhouette blanche se détache sur le bleu éclatant du
ciel de Majorque tel un phare en forme de cube qui veillerait
sur le port. L'intérieur est un mélange harmonieux de
modernisme scandinave et espagnol. Certains éléments du
mobilier et des installations des années 1950 ont été restaurés, mais l'intérieur a été en grande partie réaménagé et complète les lignes sobres et classiques de l'architecture. La vaste
piscine et le solarium, construits en même temps que l'hôtel,
ont été luxueusement rénovés et forment un cadre élégant
pour la détente.
Bien que l'une des nombreuses plages de l'île touristique ne
se trouve qu'à quelques mètres de l'hôtel, et la vieille ville
animée de Palma à deux kilomètres seulement, on ne pourrait
s'étonner que les hôtes du Portixol préfèrent ne pas quitter
son décor raffiné.
Livre à emporter: « Un Hiver à Majorque » de George Sand

ANREISE	1,5 km von Palma de Mallorca entfernt
PREIS	€
ZIMMER	25 Zimmer und Suiten
KÜCHE	Vor allem für seine moderne mediterrane Küche berühmtes Restaurant
GESCHICHTE	Gebaut und eröffnet 1956, modernisiert 1999
X-FAKTOR	Stil und Sonne

ACCÈS	À 1,5 km de Palma de Majorque
PRIX	€
CHAMBRES	25 chambres et suites
RESTAURATION	Restaurant réputé, en particulier pour sa cuisine méditerranéenne moderne
HISTOIRE	Construit et ouvert en 1956, modernisé en 1999
LES « PLUS »	Raffinement et soleil

Silence Is Golden...
Finca Son Gener, Mallorca

Finca Son Gener, Mallorca

Silence Is Golden

Rural life has many rewards; one of the best is silence. And although the crowing of a rooster or the bleating of sheep may break that silence now and then, the peace and quiet that rules here is a treat in our noisy world.

On the island of Majorca, there is the chance to lead a simple country life for a few days. Some of the most beautiful places here are set in idyllic landscapes just near the coast, and often hidden behind thick natural stone walls. The country estate of Son Gener is one of these havens. Built in the 18th century, and used for making oils and grains, it has been totally restored. The classic finca – farm – is on the eastern side of the island, on the brow of a small hill, with a view of the village, sea, and mountains. Surrounded by green fields, olive and almond trees, this is a dream domain to bask in. While the estate's simple style is in keeping with its tranquil backdrop, it has been refurbished with skill. The soft rich colours that make up the interiors are in themselves conducive to a sense of calm. The elegant house calls to mind the patrician life of past days. Those who are privileged to be guests here will be content with their choice for a pastoral interlude.

Book to pack: "Goya" by Lion Feuchtwanger

Finca Son Gener	
Cta. Vella Son Servera-Artà km3	
07550 Son Servera	
Majorca	
Spain	
Tel: + 34 971 183612	
Fax: + 34 871 70 60 16	
E-mail: hotel@songener.com	
Website: www.songener.com	

DIRECTIONS	Between the towns of Son Servera and Artà, 70 km/44 m east from Palma de Mallorca, 20 km/12 m northeast from Manacor
RATES	€€
ROOMS	10 suites
FOOD	On request, Majorcan dishes made with homegrown organic produce are served
HISTORY	Built in the 18th century, the finca was turned into a hotel in 1998
X-FACTOR	Outdoor and indoor serenity

Himmlische Ruhe

Das Landleben hat viele Vorzüge, aber einer der größten ist die Stille. Und auch wenn sie gelegentlich durch das Krähen eines Hahns oder das Blöken eines Schafs unterbrochen wird, herrscht doch meist Ruhe und Frieden – ein Luxus in unserer lauten Welt.

Auf der Insel Mallorca haben Sie Gelegenheit, für einige Tage dem einfachen Landleben zu frönen. Einige der schönsten Unterkünfte finden sich hier inmitten idyllischer Landschaften nahe der Küste, oft versteckt hinter dicken Mauern aus Naturstein. Unter ihnen ist auch der Landsitz von Son Gener, eine klassische Finca, wie hier die Bauernhöfe genannt werden, die auf der Ostseite der Insel auf der Kuppe eines kleinen Hügels liegt. Umgeben von grünen Feldern, Olivenhainen und Mandelbäumen finden Sie hier ein traumhaftes Urlaubsziel. Das im 18. Jahrhundert ursprünglich für die Öl- und Getreideproduktion gebaute Haus wurde komplett und mit großem Können renoviert. Davon zeugt der einfache Stil des Hauses, welcher sich harmonisch in die Umgebung einpasst. Zur allgemeinen Atmosphäre der Ruhe tragen die sanften, satten Farben im Hausinneren bei. Das elegante Haus weckt Erinnerungen an das Leben des gehobenen Bürgertums in früheren Zeiten.

Wer das Privileg genießt, an diesem Ort Gast zu sein, wird mit seiner Wahl dieser ländlichen Oase der Ruhe mehr als zufrieden sein.

Buchtipp: »Goya oder der arge Weg der Erkenntnis« von Lion Feuchtwanger

Le silence est d'or

La vie à la campagne a de nombreux avantages, en particulier le silence. Dans notre monde bruyant, cette paix et cette tranquillité, seulement interrompues de temps à autre par le cri d'un coq ou le bêlement d'un mouton, constituent un plaisir authentique.

Dans l'île de Majorque, on peut, le temps d'un séjour, goûter à la vie campagnarde simple. Ici, certaines des plus belles villégiatures se cachent souvent derrière d'épais murs de pierre, dans des cadres idylliques, à proximité du littoral. Le domaine de Son Gener est l'un de ces havres de paix. Construit au XVIIIe siècle, à l'origine destiné au pressage de l'huile et à la culture des céréales, il a été entièrement restauré. Cette finca (ferme) traditionnelle est située dans la partie orientale de l'île, au sommet d'une petite colline. Entourée de champs verdoyants, d'oliviers et d'amandiers, c'est un lieu de détente rêvé. Si le style simple du domaine s'harmonise avec son cadre rustique, celui-ci a été rénové avec goût. Les couleurs riches et douces des intérieurs favorisent l'impression de sérénité. L'élégante maison principale évoque la vie patricienne d'antan.

Les privilégiés qui auront la chance de séjourner à Son Gener seront ravis du choix de leur interlude champêtre.

Livre à emporter : « Goya » de Lion Feuchtwanger

ANREISE	Zwischen den Städten Son Servera und Artà, 70 km östlich von Palma, 20 km nordöstlich von Manacor
PREIS	€€
ZIMMER	10 Suiten
KÜCHE	Auf Anfrage werden inseltypische Gerichte mit Zutaten aus eigenem biologischem Anbau serviert
GESCHICHTE	Das Gebäude stammt aus dem 18. Jahrhundert und ist seit 1998 Hotel
X-FAKTOR	Entspannte Atmosphäre in Haus und Umgebung

ACCÈS	Entre les villes de Son Servera et Artà, à 70 km à l'est de Palma, à 20 km au nord-est de Manacor
PRIX	€€
CHAMBRES	10 suites
RESTAURATION	Sur demande, plats majorquins préparés avec des produits bio cultivés sur place
HISTOIRE	Construit au XVIIIe siècle, le bâtiment est un hôtel depuis 1998
LES « PLUS »	Sérénité intérieure et extérieure

Life on Mars?...
Hotel Aire de Bardenas, Tudela

Hotel Aire de Bardenas, Tudela

Life on Mars?

From a distance, the cube-shaped buildings with their aluminium façades that form the hotel complex, look like a futuristic colony; the reddish sand, characteristic of the barren landscape of Navarra in northern Spain, does the rest; or as David Bowie puts it in his song: Is there life on Mars?

In the one-storey complex there is a total of 22 rooms and suites – guaranteeing a generous ceiling height. In addition, the individual houses are uniquely aligned to the sun and the line of the horizon, so as to create the illusion that you are in a luxurious hermitage.

It's a dream that you can lose yourself in at any time, in the cool shade of the restaurant or out on the patio. The seemingly barren land of Navarra is a wine-growing region of worldwide renown, and the fertile farmland of the neighbouring region of Ribera is viewed by Spanish gourmets as a vegetable paradise. The lettuce hearts from nearby Tudela are a special delicacy!

The mid-century design classics by Charles Eames found here show off their pioneering shapes, in front of the metal cubes in the red dust. Add to this the starry sky, and you'll feel ten thousand light years from home.

Book to pack: "The House of Bernada Alba" by Federico Garcia Lorca

Hotel Aire de Bardenas
Ctra. De Ejea, 15 km
31500 Tudela
Spain
Tel: + 34 (0) 948 11 66 66
Fax: + 34 (0) 948 11 63 48
E-mail: info@hotelairedebardenas.com
www.airedebardenas.com
Open all year

DIRECTIONS	40 minutes' drive north of the airport in Zaragoza, 2 hours' drive from Bilbao or Biarritz
RATES	€€
ROOMS	22 rooms, some with private patios or views over the desert of the Bardenas Reales Natural Park and Biosphere
FOOD	It is cooked with vegetables from the hotel's own garden; the focus is on vegetarian dishes! Victoria Beckham's favourite dish is zucchini strips fried with garlic
HISTORY	The hotel was built by Mónica Rivera and Emiliano López and opened in 2007
X-FACTOR	star-gazing in the clear desert air!

Life on Mars?

Von Weitem wirken die würfelförmigen Gebäude mit ihren Aluminiumfassaden, aus denen sich der Hotelkomplex zusammensetzt, wie eine futuristische Kolonie; der rötliche Sand, charakteristisch für die karge Landschaft der Navarra im Norden Spaniens tut sein Übriges, oder wie David Bowie singt: Is there Life on Mars?

In den einstöckigen Häusern sind insgesamt 22 Zimmer und Suiten untergebracht – was eine wunderbare Deckenhöhe garantiert. Zudem sind die einzelnen Häuser individuell an Sonnenstand und den Verlauf des Horizontes ausgerichtet, sodass die Illusion entsteht, man befände sich hier in einer luxuriösen Eremitage.

Ein Traum, der sich im schattigen Restaurant, wahlweise auch auf dessen Terrasse zu jeder Zeit zerstreuen lässt. Der vermeintlich karge Landstrich der Navarra ist ein Weinanbaugebiet von weltweitem Renommee, und das fruchtbare Ackerland der benachbarten Region Ribera wird von spanischen Feinschmeckern als Gemüseparadies gehandelt. Besonders die Salatherzen aus dem nahen Tudela sind eine Delikatesse!

Die klassischen Midcentury-Designklassiker von Charles Eames stellen gerade hier, vor den Metallkuben im roten Staub, ihre zukunftsweisende Formgebung unter Beweis. Wenn dann noch der Sternenhimmel angeknipst wird, fühlt man sich zehntausend Lichtjahre von zu Hause entfernt.

Buchtipp: »Bernada Albas Haus: Tragödie von den Frauen in den Dörfern Spaniens« von Federico García Lorca

Life on Mars?

De loin, les maisons cubiques aux façades en aluminium qui composent le complexe hôtelier font penser à une colonie futuriste ; le rouge du sable, typique de ce paysage aride de Navarre, dans le nord de l'Espagne, fait le reste, ou comme le chante David Bowie : Is there Life on Mars?

Les maisons d'un étage abritent 22 chambres et suites — pour une superbe hauteur sous plafond garantie. Elles sont orientées différemment selon la position du soleil et la ligne de l'horizon, ce qui donne l'illusion de se trouver dans un luxueux ermitage.

Le rêve est dissipé dès le premier instant dans le restaurant ombragé, ou au choix sur sa terrasse : la contrée apparemment pauvre de Navarre est en réalité un vignoble de renommée mondiale, et les terres agricoles fertiles de la région voisine de Ribera sont considérées par les gourmets espagnols comme le paradis des légumes — les cœurs de salade de la ville toute proche de Tudela en particulier sont un mets de choix !

Les classiques du design Midcentury de Charles Eames prouvent ici mieux que nulle part ailleurs, dans la poussière rouge devant les cubes métalliques, leur conformation d'avenir. Si en plus le ciel allume toutes ses étoiles, on se sent à dix mille années-lumière de chez soi.

Livre à emporter : « La Maison de Bernada Alba : tragédie des femmes dans les villages d'Espagne » de Federico Garcia Lorca

ANREISE	40 min Fahrt nördlich vom Flughafen in Saragossa, 2 Std. Fahrt von Bilbao oder Biarritz	
PREIS	€€	
ZIMMER	22 Zimmer, teils mit eigenem Patio oder Aussichten in die Wüste des Bardenas-Reales-Nationalparks und -Biosphärenreservats	
KÜCHE	Es wird mit Gemüse aus dem hauseigenen Garten gekocht, der Schwerpunkt liegt auf vegetarischen Gerichten! Victoria Beckhams Lieblingsgericht sind die mit Knoblauch gebratenen Zucchinistreifen	
GESCHICHTE	Das Hotel wurde von Mónica Rivera und Emiliano López gebaut und 2007 eröffnet	
X-FAKTOR	Sterneschauen bei klarer Wüstenluft!	

ACCÈS	À 40 mn de route au nord de l'aéroport de Saragosse, 2 heures de route de Bilbao ou Biarritz	
PRIX	€€	
CHAMBRES	22 chambres, certaines avec patio ou vues sur le désert du parc national des Bardenas Reales et sa biosphère.	
RESTAURATION	La cuisine est faite avec des légumes du jardin et met l'accent sur les plats végétariens! Le plat préféré de Victoria Beckham sont les rubans de courgettes sautés à l'ail	
HISTOIRE	L'hôtel a été construit par Mónica Rivera et Emiliano López et ouvert en 2007	
LES « PLUS »	Regarder les étoiles dans l'air clair du désert !	

Noble Sacrifice...
Casa Palacio de Carmona, Sevilla

Casa Palacio de Carmona, Sevilla

Noble Sacrifice

Here is your chance to live life like a Spanish aristocrat. And if you are one already, then you'll feel right at home. Those who take care of you at Casa Palacio de Carmona, a palace now transformed into a fine hotel, will let you pretend – for a while. When you pass through the massive door of this 16th-century house, one that was home for more than four hundred years to one dynasty, you will find yourself back in nobler times. It will be easy to grow used to living in these lavish surroundings. And no doubt you will soon become accustomed to the splendid food. While others tend to the chores, you will be free to breathe in the fresh mountain air, survey the gardens, and rest in the courtyards, shaded from the sunlight. Your tasks will be to inhale the scent of the orange trees and the jasmine; listen to the silence, the murmur of the fountains, and the singing of the birds.

The palace is in the heart of the town of Carmona, said to be one of the oldest settlements in Spain. It has seen the rise and fall of successive empires. As a result, some of the most stunning Roman and Renaissance architecture in the country is to be found here.

Book to pack: "Don Quixote" by Miguel de Cervantes

Casa Palacio de Carmona
Plaza de Lazzo, 1
Carmona
41410 Seville
Spain
Tel: + 34 954 191 000
Fax: + 34 954 190 189
E-mail: reserve@casacarmona.com
Website: www.casadecarmona.com

DIRECTIONS	About 37 km/23 m east of Seville
RATES	€€
ROOMS	31 rooms, 1 suite
FOOD	Traditional Spanish cuisine with a contemporary twist
HISTORY	The Casa was built in 1561. Renovated between 1986 and 1991 it has been a hotel since then
X-FACTOR	Leading the lifestyle of a lord and lady

Ein nobles Opfer

Leben Sie ein paar Tage wie ein spanischer Adliger!
Das äußerst zuvorkommende Personal der Casa Palacio de
Carmona, eines ehemaligen Palasts, der in ein Hotel umge-
wandelt wurde, wird Sie – wenigstens für kurze Zeit – darin
unterstützen. Wenn Sie durch das mächtige Portal des aus
dem 16. Jahrhundert stammenden Prachtbaus treten, der
mehr als vierhundert Jahre von einem Adelsgeschlecht
bewohnt wurde, werden Sie sich sogleich in größere Zeiten
zurückversetzt fühlen. Gewiss wird es Ihnen nicht schwer
fallen, sich in diesem luxuriösen Ambiente einzuleben, und
auch an das köstliche Essen werden Sie sich sehr bald
gewöhnen. Während die anderen die Hausarbeit erledigen,
können Sie in den Bergen die gute Luft genießen, die Gärten
bewundern oder sich im schattigen Innenhof entspannen.
Ihre einzige Pflicht besteht darin, den Duft der Orangenbäume und Jasmine einzuatmen und der Stille, dem leisen
Plätschern des Brunnens und dem Zwitschern der Vögel zu
lauschen.
Der Palast liegt im Herzen der Stadt Carmona, einer der
ältesten Ortschaften Spaniens, die noch heute von der Blüte
und dem Untergang aufeinander folgender Königreiche
zeugt. Hier befinden sich die schönsten Bauwerke der
Romanik und der Renaissance von ganz Spanien.
Buchtipp: »Don Quijote« von Miguel de Cervantes

Noblesse oblige

Offrez-vous le luxe, pendant quelques jours, de vivre à la
manière d'un aristocrate espagnol. Si vous appartenez à la
noblesse, alors vous vous sentirez ici comme chez vous.
Vos hôtes de la Casa Palacio de Carmona, un palais transformé en hôtel de luxe, vous donneront le change... le temps
d'un court séjour. À peine aurez-vous franchi la porte massive de cette demeure du XVIe siècle, qui a abrité une seule
dynastie pendant plus de quatre cents ans, que vous vous
croirez transporté à l'époque des seigneurs. Mais vous vous
adapterez sans aucun doute rapidement à l'environnement
luxueux, et plus encore à la cuisine succulente. Tandis que le
personnel s'affaire, libre à vous de flâner dans les jardins ou
de vous reposer dans les cours ombragées en respirant l'air
frais des montagnes. Votre tâche se limitera à inhaler le parfum des orangers et des jasmins, ou encore à écouter le
silence, le murmure des fontaines et le chant des oiseaux.
Le palais est situé au cœur de Carmona, l'une des plus
vieilles villes d'Espagne. Témoin de la grandeur et de la déca-
dence de plusieurs empires, cette cité abrite quelques-unes
des plus belles architectures de style roman et Renaissance
du pays.
Livre à emporter : « Don Quichotte » de Miguel de Cervantès

ANREISE	Etwa 37 km östlich von Sevilla
PREIS	€€
ZIMMER	31 Zimmer und 1 Suite
KÜCHE	Traditionelle spanische Küche mit modernem Einschlag
GESCHICHTE	Die Casa wurde 1561 erbaut. Nach ihrer Renovierung von 1986 und 1991 wurde sie als Hotel eröffnet
X-FAKTOR	Leben wie ein Edelmann oder eine Edelfrau

ACCÈS	À 37 km environ à l'est de Séville
PRIX	€€
CHAMBRES	31 chambres et 1 suite
RESTAURATION	Cuisine traditionnelle espagnole, aux accents contemporains
HISTOIRE	La Casa a été construite en 1561 et reconvertie en hôtel après une rénovation de 1986 à 1991
LES « PLUS »	Vivre en grand seigneur

Architecture Meets Nature...
Pousada de Amares, Santa Maria do Bouro

Pousada de Amares, Santa Maria do Bouro

Architecture Meets Nature

The former Cistercian monastery dating from the 12th century was rebuilt to plans by Pritzker Prize winner Eduardo Souto de Moura in the 1990s. With their strict asceticism and spirituality, their art and craft, the Cistercians were one of the most influential religious orders in the Middle Ages. They created monasteries of sublime austerity, and religious buildings to foster mental clarity and purity. Where monks once lived in barren cells, guests at Pousado Santa Maria do Bouro now have minimalist rooms and suites at their disposal.

Huge floor-to-ceiling windows provide views over the mountains. The medieval building still retains its massiveness and beautiful proportions, which even now instill a sense of shelter. But a sensitive reworking of the foundations has removed any sense of severity. This is particularly evident in the stairwells. The sculptural elegance of the raw stone was laid bare and, from a haven of silence, a temple of peace was created. The furnishing is simply accentuated by the classic "model 209" chair by Thonet, which looks as if it had been specially created for the stone vaults of the restaurant. Le Corbusier favoured this classic 1900 design for his sculptural concrete architecture. At dinner there, when the reflection of the flickering candles dances over the 800-year-old stone pillars, a magical and truly modern effect is produced.

Book to pack: "The Gospel According to Jesus Christ" by José Saramago

Pousada de Amares

Hotel Santa Maria de Bouro

Santa Maria do Bouro

4720-633 Amares

Portugal

Tel: + 35 (0) 125 882 175 1

E-mail: reservas@pousadasofportugal.com

www.pousadasofportugal.com

DIRECTIONS	79 km north of the airport in Porto between Braga, the religious capital of Portugal, and Peneda Gerês National Park
RATES	€
ROOMS	32 rooms including 2 suites
FOOD	A restaurant serves regional specialties. In the bar and on the terrace with views of the mountains you can enjoy the excellent local Vinho Verde
HISTORY	The monastery was built in the 12th century by the Cistercians, rebuilt 1994–1997 by Eduardo Souto de Moura and then opened as a Pousada hotel
X-FACTOR	The magnificent architecture and landscape!

Architektur trifft Natur

Das ehemalige Zisterzienserkloster aus dem 12. Jahrhundert wurde nach Plänen des Pritzker-Preisträgers Eduardo Souta de Moura in den 1990er-Jahren umgebaut. Mit ihrer strengen Spiritualität und Askese, Technik und Handwerk wurden die Zisterzienser im Hochmittelalter zu einem der einflussreichsten Orden. Sie schufen Klöster von erhabener Schmucklosigkeit und Sakralbauten für geistige Klarheit und Reinheit. Wo einst Mönche in kargen Zellen lebten, stehen den Gästen der Pousado Santa Maria do Bouro nun minimalistisch eingerichtete Zimmer und Suiten zur Verfügung. Riesige bodentief eingesetzte Fenster geben den Blick frei auf die Berge. Die Wuchtigkeit und schönen Proportionen des mittelalterlichen Bauwerks, die für uns heute auch etwas Bergendes haben, sind dem Gebäude belassen worden. Doch wurde ihnen durch die sensible Neuaufteilung der Grundrisse jegliche Schwere genommen. Dies zeigt sich insbesondere in den Treppenhäusern. Freigelegt wurde die skulpturale Eleganz des rohen Steins. Aus einem Hort des Schweigens wurde ein Tempel der Ruhe gemacht. Der Möblierung bleibt hier lediglich noch zu akzentuieren, der klassische Stuhl „Modell 209" von Thonet wirkt hier wie geschaffen für die steinernen Gewölbe des Restaurants. Schon Le Corbusier favorisierte diesen Klassiker aus dem Jahr 1900 für seine skulpturale Betonarchitektur. Bei einem Dinner dort, wenn der Widerschein flackernder Kerzen an den 800 Jahre alten Steinsäulen tanzt, ergibt sich ein magischer, ein wahrhaft moderner Effekt.

Buchtipp: »Das Evangelium nach Jesus Christus« von José Saramago

Symbiose entre architecture et nature

L'ancien couvent cistercien du XIIe siècle a été transformé dans les années 1990 d'après des plans de l'architecte lauréat du prix Pritzker Eduardo Souta de Moura. Les cisterciens, leur spiritualité sévère et leur ascèse, leur travail et leur artisanat, étaient l'un des ordres les plus influents pendant le haut Moyen Âge. Ils ont construit des couvents d'une simplicité et d'un dépouillement sublimes, ainsi que des bâtiments sacrés pour la clarté et la pureté de l'âme. Les austères cellules des moines d'autrefois sont aujourd'hui des chambres et des suites au mobilier minimaliste, à la disposition des clients de la Pousada Santa Maria do Bouro. D'immenses fenêtres au ras du sol ouvrent une vue parfaitement dégagée sur les montagnes. L'imposant édifice moyenâgeux aux belles proportions a été conservé, il a pour nous aujourd'hui quelque chose de secret. Le redécoupage plein de sensibilité lui a cependant pris toute gravité, comme on le voit notamment aux escaliers. L'élégance sculpturale de la pierre brute a été dégagée et le havre du silence a fait place à un sanctuaire du calme. Le mobilier n'a été placé que pour accentuer encore le caractère de l'endroit : la chaise classique « 209 » de Thonet semble comme faite pour les voûtes de pierre du restaurant. Le Corbusier lui aussi avait privilégié ce modèle classique de 1900 pour son architecture sculpturale de béton. Les dîners à la lueur vacillante des bougies qui danse sur les colonnes de pierre vieilles de 800 ans s'y déroulent dans une atmosphère magique, mais véritablement moderne.

Livre à emporter : « L'Évangile selon Jésus-Christ » de José Saramago

ANREISE	79 km nördlich vom Flughafen in Porto zwischen Braga, der religiösen Hauptstadt Portugals, und dem Peneda-Geres-Nationalpark gelegen
PREIS	€
ZIMMER	32 Zimmer, davon 2 Suiten
KÜCHE	Ein Restaurant serviert Spezialitäten der Region. In der Bar und auf der Terrasse mit Ausblicken auf die Berge genießt man den exzellenten, hiesigen Vinho Verde
GESCHICHTE	Das Kloster wurde im 12. Jahrhundert von den Zisterziensern gebaut, 1994 bis 1997 von Eduardo Souto de Moura umgebaut und dann als Pousada-Hotel eröffnet
X-FAKTOR	die großartige Architektur und Landschaft!

ACCÈS	À 79 km au nord de l'aéroport de Porto, entre Braga, la capitale religieuse du Portugal, et le parc national Peneda Geres
PRIX	€
CHAMBRES	32 chambres, dont 2 suites
RESTAURATION	Un restaurant sert des spécialités régionales. On peut déguster l'excellent vinho verde local au bar et sur la terrasse avec vue sur les montagnes
HISTOIRE	Le couvent a été construit au XIIe siècle par les cisterciens, transformé de 1994 à 1997 par Eduardo Souto de Moura et ouvert en tant qu'hôtel Pousada
LES « PLUS »	Architecture et paysage fantastiques !

Somewhere in Time...
Palace Hotel da Curia, Tamengos

Palace Hotel da Curia, Tamengos

Somewhere in Time

In the 1920s, this was a splendid new hotel. One of the last grand Art Nouveau buildings in Europe, it was quite the most stylish place when it first welcomed guests through its doors. It was set in magnificent gardens, in an elegant Portuguese spa town; one to which high-society people came to take the so-called healing waters. Luckily, the Palace Hotel da Curia is as lovely now as it was back then. Time seems to have stood still here. The atmosphere is much as it used to be.

Although it has been restored, you can see what it must have been like over half a century ago. Wisely, little has been changed; it has been kept looking much as it did in the old days. New comforts have been added, but all the chic of that golden era remains. Yet this stately old hotel is still a new landmark in a region that is steeped in history.

The Beiras near the Atlantic Ocean is a lesser known part of Portugal and is rather off the beaten track. Its surroundings range from mountains to lush valleys, from quiet villages to long, curving beaches. Though it may be short on attention, it is rich in variety.

Book to pack: "Journey to Portugal" by José Saramago

Palace Hotel da Curia

Curia 3780-541
Tamengos
Portugal
Tel: + 351 231 510 300
Fax: +351 231 515 31
E-mail: curiapalace@themahotels.pt
Website: www.curiapalace.com,
www.themahotels.pt

DIRECTIONS	20 km/12 m north of Coimbra; 2 hours north from Lisbon, and an hour south from Porto
RATES	€
ROOMS	114 rooms
FOOD	Local specialities and classic international cuisine
HISTORY	Built in the early 1920s, the Palace Hotel da Curia opened in 1926. Complete renovation, concluded in 2008, reinforced the historical character of the place and added a boutique spa
X-FACTOR	Belle Époque flair

Eine andere Zeit

Erbaut in den 1920er-Jahren, gehörte das Hotel zu den letzten großen Jugendstilbauten Europas und galt, als es seine ersten Gäste willkommen hieß, als Verkörperung wahren Stils. Es lag in einer prachtvollen Gartenanlage, in einem eleganten Kurort, wo sich die High Society an den heilenden Quellen labte. Glücklicherweise scheint im Palace Hotel da Curia die Zeit stehen geblieben zu sein, sodass man förmlich die zauberhafte Atmosphäre vergangener Tage spürt. Obwohl das Hotel inzwischen renoviert wurde, kann man sich genau vorstellen, wie es hier vor mehr als einem halben Jahrhundert zuging. Denn es wurde klugerweise nur wenig verändert. Natürlich ist moderner Komfort hinzugekommen, doch der Flair des Goldenen Zeitalters blieb erhalten. Und man darf eines nicht vergessen: Inmitten dieser durch und durch historischen Landschaft ist das ehrwürdige alte Hotel immer noch ein relativ neues Wahrzeichen.

Die Landschaft Beiras an der Atlantikküste Portugals gehört zu den weniger bekannten Regionen, in die sich nicht jeder »verirrt«. Dabei ist sie eine der abwechslungsreichsten des Landes. Hier finden sich Bergzüge neben üppig begrünten Tälern, stille Dörfchen und lange Strände.

Buchtipp: »Hoffnung im Alentejo« von José Saramago

Réminiscences

Dans les années 1920, c'était un hôtel Art nouveau flambant neuf ; l'un de ces établissements élégants où se côtoyait l'élite européenne. Entouré d'un magnifique jardin, il se dressait dans une ville portugaise alors très sélect, réputée pour ses eaux thermales curatives. Par bonheur, le Palace Hotel da Curia a su garder son charme et son atmosphère d'antan. Ici, le temps semble s'être arrêté.

Bien que l'hôtel ait été restauré, il a fort heureusement subi peu de changements et offre la même ambiance qui y régnait il y a près de cent ans. Si l'on y trouve aujourd'hui tout le confort moderne, il a su conserver le cachet typique de la Belle Époque. Désormais d'un autre siècle, ce palace majestueux reste néanmoins une création encore bien jeune dans cette région gorgée d'histoire.

Beiras sur la côte atlantique est une des contrées les moins connues du Portugal, encore hors des sentiers battus. Située sur la côte occidentale, elle fait partie des régions les plus diversifiées du pays, alliant montagnes et vallées verdoyantes, villages paisibles et longs rivages de sable.

Livre à emporter : « Histoire du siège de Lisbonne » de José Saramago

ANREISE	20 km nördlich von Coimbra, 2 Stunden nördlich von Lissabon und 1 Stunde südlich von Porto entfernt
PREIS	€
ZIMMER	114 Zimmer
KÜCHE	Lokale Spezialitäten und klassische internationale Küche
GESCHICHTE	Erbaut in den 1920er Jahren, eröffnet 1926
X-FAKTOR	Flair der Belle Époque

ACCÈS	À 20 km au nord de Coïmbra; à 2 heures au nord de Lisbonne et 1 heure au sud de Porto
PRIX	€
CHAMBRES	114 chambres
RESTAURATION	Spécialités locales et cuisine internationale
HISTOIRE	Construit au début des années 1920, l'hôtel a ouvert en 1926. La rénovation intégrale, achevée en 2008, souligne le caractère historique de l'endroit, complété par une boutique spa
LES «PLUS»	Ambiance Belle Époque

Pilgrim's Rest...

Paço de São Cipriano, Minho

Paço de São Cipriano, Minho

Pilgrim's Rest

This house would have been a welcome sight to pilgrims on their way to the cathedral and shrine of St. James, in Spain. For centuries, thousands of people have trod this road on a journey to see the tomb of the Apostle. Walking the long route to Santiago de Compostela, from France through Portugal and then on to Spain, was a spiritual goal. The sore feet on such a trek was likely a sharp daily reminder of one's human frailties. Resting at Paço de São Cipriano would have been a divine treat to look forward to. It still is for many. The ancient custom of receiving guests carries on; the modern traveller or the pilgrim, by car or on foot, is still welcomed here. This former manor house is set in the midst of lush greenery. As well as gardens, orchards, and vineyards, it has its own chapel, and is also blessed with wine cellars. The house is one of the many old noble seats that have been restored all through the country. While most are still family homes, paying guests can now share their proud history. The past is very much part of the present. Here, the tower room, with its splendid bed, evokes the spirit of the old Portugal.

Book to pack: "The Pilgrimage: A Contemporary Quest for Ancient Wisdom" by Paulo Coelho

Paço de São Cipriano	
Tabuadelo 4810-892	
Guimarães	
Minho	
Portugal	
Tel: + 351 253 565 337	
Fax: + 351 253 565 337	
E-Mail: info@pacoscipriano.com	
Website: www.pacoscipriano.com	

DIRECTIONS	In the north of Portugal, north-east from Porto. 6 km from Guimarães
RATES	€
ROOMS	7 rooms
FOOD	Only breakfast, restaurants near the hotel
HISTORY	The house was built in the 15th century and opened as a hotel in 1983
X-FACTOR	The serene gardens and sense of history

Nachtlager für Pilger

Dieses Haus wäre ein willkommener Anblick für Pilger auf dem Weg zur Kathedrale des heiligen Jakobus in Spanien gewesen. Im Laufe der Jahrhunderte sind tausende von Menschen hier entlang gepilgert, um das Grabmal des Apostels zu sehen. Der weite Weg nach Santiago de Compostela von Frankreich über Portugal bis nach Spanien war ein großes religiöses Ereignis. Und die vom langen Marsch wunden Füsse gemahnten die Menschen täglich an ihre Gebrechlichkeit. Sich im Paço de São Cipriano zur Ruhe zu legen wäre gewiss ein göttliches Vergnügen gewesen, dem man mit großer Freude entgegengeblickt hätte. Viele können das heute noch genießen, denn der alte Brauch, Gäste zu empfangen, wird fortgeführt. Jeder – vom modernen Reisenden bis zum Pilger, egal, ob mit dem Auto oder zu Fuß – ist hier willkommen.

Das ehemalige Herrenhaus ist eingebettet in eine üppige, grüne Landschaft. Neben Gärten, Obstgärten und Weinbergen verfügt es über eine eigene Kapelle und ist noch dazu mit Weinkellern bestückt. Es handelt sich um einen der vielen alten Adelssitze, die im ganzen Land restauriert wurden. Obwohl die meisten von ihnen noch im Familienbesitz sind, können auch zahlende Gäste an ihrer stolzen Geschichte teilhaben. Die Vergangenheit ist in der Gegenwart noch sehr präsent. So lässt das Turmzimmer mit seinem prächtigen Bett den Geist des alten Portugals auferstehen.

Buchtipp: »Auf dem Jakobsweg. Tagebuch einer Pilgerreise nach Santiago de Compostela« von Paulo Coelho

Sur la route des pèlerins

Nul doute que la vue de cette maison n'ait réjoui bien des pèlerins en route vers la cathédrale Saint-Jacques en Espagne. Au cours des siècles, des milliers de personnes ont parcouru le chemin menant à la tombe de l'apôtre. La route de Compostelle, de la France à l'Espagne en passant par le Portugal, avait une finalité spirituelle. Les pieds meurtris rappelaient chaque jour la fragilité de l'homme. Faire enfin halte au Paço de São Cipriano devait être un moment divin... et l'est toujours aujourd'hui. L'ancienne coutume d'accueillir les voyageurs perdure : touriste ou pèlerin, en voiture ou à pied, chacun est ici le bienvenu. Cet ancien manoir est situé au cœur d'une nature verdoyante. Outre des jardins, vergers et vignobles, il possède sa propre chapelle et des caves à vin. La demeure fait partie des nombreuses résidences patriciennes à avoir été restaurées dans le pays. Si la plupart sont toujours habitées par les familles d'origine, des hôtes payants peuvent partager leur fier passé. L'histoire semble faire partie du présent : ici, la chambre de la tour, avec son lit splendide, évoque le Portugal au temps jadis.

Livre à emporter : « Le Pèlerin de Compostelle » de Paulo Coelho

ANREISE	Im Norden von Portugal, nordöstlich von Porto, 6 km von Guimarães entfernt
PREIS	€
ZIMMER	7 Zimmer
KÜCHE	Nur Frühstück, Restaurants in der Nähe des Hotels
GESCHICHTE	Das Gebäude stammt aus dem 15. Jahrhundert und wurde 1983 als Hotel eröffnet
X-FAKTOR	Die herrlichen Gärten und der Sinn für Geschichte

ACCÈS	Au nord du Portugal, au nord-est de Porto. À 6 km de Guimarães
PRIX	€
CHAMBRES	7 chambres
RESTAURATION	Petit déjeuner uniquement, restaurants à proximité de l'hôtel
HISTOIRE	Construit au XVe siècle, le Paço de São Cipriano a ouvert ses portes en 1983
LES « PLUS »	Jardins paisibles et cadre historique

Grace and Favour...
Belmond Reid's Palace, Madeira

Belmond Reid's Palace, Madeira

Grace and Favour

For generations this grand old hotel has been the epitome of grace. Belmond Reid's Palace has served as a home away from home to many of the most well-known people of the last century. The guest book is a roll call of celebrities. Anybody who was, or is still, somebody has stayed here at one time. So little seems to have changed that one might picture Winston Churchill taking afternoon tea on the terrace; Elisabeth, the Empress of Austria, gazing out to sea from her veranda; or imagine watching George Bernard Shaw being taught the tango on the lawn. The old-fashioned charm continues to draw the rich and famous, as well as the not yet renowned. Part of the attraction is the setting on the island of Madeira. High up on the clifftops overlooking the Bay of Funchal and the Atlantic, the hotel's site adds to the privacy of its guests. Staying here is almost like being on the "grand tour"; but the days of luxury travel are not re-created here, in fact it has always been like this.

Belmond Reid's Palace evokes eras that were more gracious and less hurried than the one we live in now. Time has been kind to this lovely old landmark.

Book to pack: "Pygmalion and My Fair Lady" by George Bernard Shaw

Belmond Reid's Palace		
Estrada Monumental 139	DIRECTIONS	22 km/14 m from Madeira International Airport
9000-098 Funchal	RATES	€€€
Madeira	ROOMS	130 rooms and 34 suites
Portugal	FOOD	5 restaurants to choose from
Tel: + 351 291 71 71 71	HISTORY	The original hotel was built and opened in 1891. In 1967 an extension was built
Fax: + 351 291 71 71 77	X-FACTOR	A destination in itself
E-mail: reservations.rds@belmond.com		
Website: www.belmond.com/reidspalace		

Ruhm und Ehre

Seit Generationen war dieses große alte Hotel der Inbegriff von Eleganz.

In Belmond Reid's Palace fanden viele berühmte Persönlichkeiten des letzten Jahrhunderts eine zweite Heimat. Alle Berühmtheiten haben – so scheint es – schon einmal hier gewohnt. Und so wenig scheinen sich die Zeiten verändert zu haben, dass man sich noch jetzt Winston Churchill beim Nachmittagstee auf der Terrasse vorstellen kann oder die österreichische Kaiserin Elisabeth, berühmt als Sisi, die von ihrer Veranda aus auf das Meer blickt, oder George Bernard Shaw, der auf dem Rasen Tango lernt. Ungebrochen scheint der altmodische Charme des Hotels wie ein Magnet auf die Reichen und Schönen zu wirken, aber ebenso auf die nicht wirklich oder noch nicht Berühmten. Ein weiterer Anziehungspunkt ist die Lage des Hotels. Hoch über den Klippen errichtet, bietet es einen Blick über die Bucht von Funchal auf den Atlantik und schützt durch seine exponierte Lage die Privatsphäre der Gäste.

Wer hier zu Gast ist, wird sich fühlen wie damals die reichen jungen Leute, die durch die Welt reisen, um ihren Horizont zu erweitern. Aber hier muss die Vergangenheit nicht künstlich wiedererweckt werden, hier ist es einfach so, wie es schon immer gewesen ist. An diesem Ort, zu dem die Zeit so freundlich war, darf man noch einmal teilhaben am Charme und der Ruhe früherer Zeiten.

Buchtipps: »Pygmalion and My Fair Lady« von George Bernard Shaw

»Churchill« von Sebastian Haffner

Retraite des célébrités

Symbole d'élégance depuis des générations, le Belmond Reid's Palace a accueilli maintes célébrités du siècle passé, comme en témoigne son livre d'or. Tous les grands personnages ont séjourné au moins une fois en ces lieux. Le cadre a si peu changé que l'on imagine sans peine Winston Churchill prendre le thé sur la terrasse, Sissi, impératrice d'Autriche, scruter la mer depuis sa véranda, ou George Bernard Shaw prendre des cours de tango sur la pelouse. Le charme désuet continue d'attirer les grands et les moins grands de ce monde. L'un des atouts de l'hôtel est sa situation sur l'île de Madère. Perché sur les falaises dominant la baie de Funchal et l'Atlantique, il offre la retraite discrète recherchée par la clientèle.

Un séjour dans ce palace évoque les somptueux voyages de la haute société d'autrefois ; mais le luxe n'a pas été recréé. Ici, il existe depuis toujours. Le Belmond Reid's Palace rappelle une époque plus raffinée et moins agitée que celle d'aujourd'hui.

Le temps a su épargner cet endroit plein de charme et de chic.

Livre à emporter : « L'Homme et les armes » de George Bernard Shaw

ANREISE	22 km vom Flughafen Madeira International
PREIS	€€€
ZIMMER	130 Zimmer und 34 Suiten
KÜCHE	5 Restaurants stehen zur Auswahl
GESCHICHTE	Das ursprüngliche Hotel wurde 1891 gebaut und eröffnet; 1967 kam ein Anbau hinzu
X-FAKTOR	Ein Ziel an sich

ACCÈS	À 22 km de l'aéroport Madeira International
PRIX	€€€
CHAMBRES	130 chambres et 34 suites
RESTAURATION	5 restaurants au choix
HISTOIRE	L'hôtel a été construit et a ouvert en 1891. Une annexe a été ajoutée en 1967
LES « PLUS »	Une destination en soi

VIEW OF
REID'S NEW HOTEL
MADEIRA.

Crossroads...
Marco Polo Mansion, Rhodos

Marco Polo Mansion, Rhodos

Crossroads

Greek myth ascribes the origin of Rhodes to the passion that sun god Helios felt for Poseidon the sea god's daughter. This love resulted in the birth of an island blessed with sun, and for centuries it has attracted all sorts of visitors to its shores. On a small street surrounded by mosques, and sequestered behind shutters, the Marco Polo Mansion is a magnet for travellers and "Rhodes scholars" alike. The hotel takes the latter part of its name from the Latin *manere*, which means to stay and to dwell. Here the atmosphere is such that guests can easily be inclined to linger for days. Hidden behind the walls of this little medieval hotel is a cool green garden. Apricot and orange trees grow alongside purple bougainvilleas and red poinsettias in a brilliant blaze of colour. Inside the arched doorways it is just as vibrant, with richly hued walls and furnishings. A mix of Mediterranean antiques and locally made pieces fashioned in the island's traditional simple style add detail.

This beautifully restored house in the old town's Turkish quarter is a perfect base from which to explore the classical island of Rhodes.

Books to pack: "The Travels of Marco Polo" by Marco Polo "The Discovery of Slowness" by Sten Nadolny

Marco Polo Mansion
42, Ag. Fanouriou
Old Town
85100 Rhodes
Greece
Tel: + 30 2410 25562
Fax: + 30 2410 25562
E-mail: marcopolomansion@hotmail.com
Website: www.marcopolomansion.com

DIRECTIONS	In the Turkish quarter of the old town of Rhodes
RATES	€
ROOMS	7 rooms, all unique, one with a traditional Turkish bath
FOOD	A cosmopolitan mix of Greek, Turkish, and Italian in this multi-ethnic town
HISTORY	The house was built in the 15th century and was opened as a hotel in 1999
X-FACTOR	Historic and beautiful hotel in the ancient town

Kreuzwege

Die griechische Mythologie führt die Entstehung von Rhodos auf die Leidenschaft des Sonnengottes Helios für die Tochter des Meeresgottes Poseidon zurück. Frucht dieser Liebe war eine von der Sonne verwöhnte Insel, die seit Jahrhunderten Besucher an ihre Ufer lockt.

In einer kleinen, von Moscheen gesäumten Straße liegt das Marco Polo Mansion, das Urlaubsreisende und Rhodos-Forscher gleichermaßen anzieht. Der letzte Teil des Hotelnamens ist von dem lateinischen Verb »manere« abgeleitet, welches so viel bedeutet wie »bleiben« oder »wohnen«. Und tatsächlich vermag die Atmosphäre dieses Ortes selbst Durchreisende zum tagelangen Verweilen zu verleiten. Versteckt hinter den Mauern dieses kleinen Hotels liegt ein schattiger grüner Garten, in dem Aprikosen- und Orangenbäume zwischen farbenprächtigen violetten Bougainvilleas und roten Weihnachtssternen wachsen. Wenn man dann durch die Torbögen ins Innere des Hauses tritt, wird man von den ebenso satten Farbtönen der Wände und Möbel bezaubert. Mediterrane Antiquitäten und regionales Kunsthandwerk, die im traditionell schnörkellosen Stil der Insel gefertigt sind, ergänzen diese Pracht.

Das mittelalterliche, kunstvoll restaurierte Haus im türkischen Viertel der Altstadt bietet einen perfekten Ausgangspunkt für die Erkundung der Insel Rhodos.

Buchtipps: »Die Reisen des Venezianers Marco Polo« von Marco Polo

»Die Entdeckung der Langsamkeit« von Sten Nadolny

Carrefour de cultures

La mythologie grecque attribue l'origine de Rhodes à la passion du dieu Soleil pour la fille de Poséidon, dieu de la Mer. Cet amour donna naissance à une île bénie du soleil, qui depuis des siècles a attiré toutes sortes de visiteurs, y compris les chevaliers hospitaliers de Saint-Jean-de-Jérusalem. Dans une ruelle entourée de mosquées, derrière ses volets, un hôtel offre une atmosphère conviviale qui séduit le voyageur. Le Marco Polo Mansion tire le dernier mot de son nom du latin «manere», qui signifie «rester» ou «séjourner», et, en effet, ses hôtes s'y attardent volontiers. Dans ses murs, ce petit hôtel médiéval cache un jardin frais et verdoyant. Des abricotiers et orangers y poussent à côté de bougainvillées pourpres et de poinsettias rouges, dans un flamboiement de couleurs éblouissantes. Au-delà des portes voûtées, les teintes riches des murs et des tentures rivalisent d'éclat avec le jardin. Des antiquités méditerranéennes et un mobilier fabriqué dans le style traditionnel de l'île s'harmonisent à l'ensemble.

Cette maison magnifiquement restaurée, située dans le quartier turc de la vieille ville, est un point de départ idéal pour l'exploration de l'île de Rhodes.

Livres à emporter : «Le Livre des merveilles. Les routes de l'Asie» par Marco Polo

«La Découverte de la lenteur» de Sten Nadolny

ANREISE	Im türkischen Viertel der Altstadt von Rhodos
PREIS	€
ZIMMER	7 Zimmer, alle individuell gestaltet, 1 mit traditionellem türkischen Bad
KÜCHE	Eine kosmopolitische Kombination aus griechischen, türkischen und italienischen Elementen im Stil dieser multikulturellen Stadt
GESCHICHTE	Im 15. Jahrhundert erbaut, 1999 als Hotel eröffnet
X-FAKTOR	Bildschönes historisches Hotel in einer geschichtsträchtigen Stadt

ACCÈS	Dans le quartier turc de la vieille ville de Rhodes
PRIX	€
CHAMBRES	7 chambres, toutes différentes, dont 1 avec bain turc traditionnel
RESTAURATION	Cuisine cosmopolite grecque, turque et italienne, dans cette ville aux ethnies diverses
HISTOIRE	Construit au XVe siècle, l'hôtel a ouvert en 1999
LES « PLUS »	Bel hôtel historique dans la vieille ville

marco polo
cafe

espresso ~ cappuccino
nescafe ~ frappe
greek coffee
fresh juices
long drinks
cocktails
beers
wines
salads
desserts
yoghurt with honey

Caving in Comfort...
Les Maisons de Cappadoce, Uçhisar

Les Maisons de Cappadoce, Uçhisar

Caving in Comfort

There are few places on earth like Cappadocia in central Turkey. Its otherworldly landscape of volcanic rock has been sculpted by time and the elements into amazing spires and needles, amongst which apple, apricot, and mulberry trees flourish in fertile valleys. The first Christians carved churches, houses, and whole subterranean cities in the soft volcanic tufa rock to escape invaders. Perched at the highest point above this bizarre landscape is the ancient hamlet of Uçhisar. Here, once dilapidated cave dwellings in the oldest part of the village, have been transformed into Les Maisons de Cappadoce, ten stone houses. Sensitively restored, their added contemporary comforts merging easily with the millennial architecture, these unique homes are available to people seeking a holiday in a truly unusual place. You can pass your time as a temporary troglodyte tasting the delicious Turkish food in the local restaurants, enjoying the hospitality of the village, and perhaps bargaining at the carpet and kilim shops. And you can follow the ancient paths of Cappadocia, walking, riding, driving, or ballooning over it, to wonder at the extraordinary terrain spread out below.

Book to pack: "Memed, My Hawk" by Yashar Kemal

Les Maisons de Cappadoce

Belediye Meydani

POB 28 Uçhisar Nevshehir

Turkey

Phone: + 90 384 219 28 13

Fax: April 1–October 31: + 90 384 219 27 82;

November 1–March 31: + 33 (0) 563 46 20 09

E-mail: info@cappadoce.com

Website: www.cappadoce.com

DIRECTIONS	300 km/180 m south-east from Ankara, 800 km/500 m south-east from Istanbul; Nevshehir is the nearest airport (40 km/25 m), or Kayseri (80 km/50 m)
RATES	€
ROOMS	11 houses, for 2 to 7 people
FOOD	Breakfast hampers available, Turkish cuisine in Uçhisar or self-catering
HISTORY	The guesthouses have been renovated in the 90s, the first opened 1994
X-FACTOR	Bewitching scenery, enchanting accommodation

Erhöhlungsurlaub

Nur wenige Regionen auf der Welt sind mit Kappadokien vergleichbar. Eine bizarre Landschaft aus Vulkangestein ist im Lauf der Jahrtausende durch die Kraft der Naturgewalten entstanden. Zwischen den eindrucksvollen Felstürmen und -nadeln aber blühen Apfel-, Aprikosen- und Maulbeerbäume in fruchtbaren Tälern. Die ersten Christen meißelten Kirchen, Häuser und ganze unterirdische Städte aus dem weichen, vulkanischen Tuffstein und versteckten sich hier vor ihren Verfolgern.

Auf dem höchsten Plateau dieser Mondlandschaft im Herzen der Türkei liegt das alte Dörfchen Uçhisar. Hier wurden einige der verlassenen Höhlenwohnungen, welche sich im ältesten Teil des Ortes befinden, zu den zehn Steinhäusern von Les Maisons de Cappadoce umgebaut. Diese einzigartigen, sehr stilvoll renovierten Häuser, in denen moderner Komfort und die mehr als tausend Jahre alte Architektur eine harmonische Verbindung eingehen, sind Traumziele für alle diejenigen, die einen absolut unkonventionellen Urlaub verbringen wollen. Als Einsiedler auf Zeit können Sie sich hier an den hervorragenden türkischen Spezialitäten in den örtlichen Restaurants erfreuen, die Gastfreundschaft der Dorfbewohner genießen und vielleicht mit den Teppichhändlern um Kelims feilschen. Die jahrtausendealten Pfade Kappadokiens können Sie zu Fuß, zu Pferde oder mit dem Auto erkunden, oder gar vom Heißluftballon aus, um die außergewöhnliche Landschaft von oben zu bestaunen.

Buchtipp: »Memed, mein Falke« von Yaçar Kemal

Grottes tout confort

Peu d'endroits sur terre égalent la Cappadoce. Des vallées fertiles où poussent des pommiers, des abricotiers et des mûriers s'étendent au pied de paysages surréels de roche volcanique, où la nature a sculpté au fil des siècles des flèches et aiguilles extraordinaires. Dans le tuf, une roche volcanique poreuse et légère, les premiers chrétiens ont creusé des églises, des maisons ainsi que des cités souterraines entières pour se protéger des envahisseurs.

Le hameau ancien d'Uçhisar est perché sur le point le plus élevé de ce paysage fantastique de Turquie centrale. Dans la partie la plus ancienne du village, des habitations troglodytiques autrefois délabrées ont été transformées en dix maisons d'hôtes : Les Maisons de Cappadoce. Restaurées avec goût, le confort moderne s'intégrant sans heurter l'architecture millénaire, ces demeures uniques séduiront ceux qui souhaitent passer des vacances dans un endroit véritablement original.

Troglodyte le temps d'un séjour, vous savourerez la délicieuse cuisine turque dans les restaurants locaux, découvrirez le village et ses habitants accueillants et vous amuserez à marchander dans les boutiques de tapis et de kilims. Vous pourrez aussi parcourir les chemins anciens de Cappadoce, à pied, à cheval ou en voiture, ou bien survoler en ballon des paysages absolument extraordinaires.

Livre à emporter : « Le dernier combat de Mèmed le Mince » de Yachar Kemal

ANREISE	300 km südöstlich von Ankara, 800 km südöstlich von Istanbul. Die nächsten Flughäfen sind Nevshehir (40 km) und Kayseri (80 km)
PREIS	€
ZIMMER	11 Häuser für 2 bis 7 Personen
KÜCHE	Selbstversorger sind willkommen, Frühstückskörbe auf Wunsch, türkische Spezialitäten gibt es in Uçhisar
GESCHICHTE	Die Häuser wurden in den 1990er Jahren renoviert, das erste 1994 eröffnet
X-FAKTOR	Fantastische Landschaft, bezaubernde Unterkünfte

ACCÈS	À 300 km au sud-est d'Ankara et à 800 km au sud-est d'Istanbul ; 2 aéroports : Nevshehir (à 40 km) ou Kayseri (à 80 km)
PRIX	€
CHAMBRES	11 maisons logeant de 2 à 7 sept personnes
RESTAURATION	Panier de petit déjeuner sur demande ; cuisine turque à Uçhisar ou possibilité de préparer soi-même ses repas
HISTOIRE	Les maison ont été rénovées dans les années 1990, la première a été ouverte en 1994
LES « PLUS »	Cadre fantastique, logement original

› **abitarelastoria.it**
accommodation in historical dwellings in
towns and in the country, in the north and
south of Italy; links to each property, with
photos and detailed information; plus interesting itineraries.

› **agriturist.it**
farm stays in the Italian countryside, country
homes restored with hospitality in mind,
serving regional food, and offering a glimpse
into rural life without having to work.

› **bedandbreakfast.com**
offbeat places to stay all over the world that
offer a different experience (but not too different) from hotels, with detailed information,
lots of photos, links to individual Websites
and on-line reservations.

› **boutiquelodging.com**
global network of independently owned hotels
and resorts, with a full list of properties on
the site.

› **castlesontheweb.com**
for history buffs, royalists and fantasists;
accommodating castles all over the world,
from King Arthur's Camelot Castle in
Cornwall to one in Jamaica, with ratings.

› **concierge.com**
the online home of Condé Nast Traveller, the
American travel magazine; with feature articles and links to "hot lists" of hotels.

› **culturaltravels.com**
lists holiday themes such as cuisine and
religion, for the culturally minded traveller,
with detailed articles and links through
to tour hosts for each themed holiday.

› **dolcevita.com**
tips and information for leading the good life
in Italy, click on travel for recommendations
on top places to stay from spas to monasteries to farm-stays; no direct links but useful
information with contact details.

› **ellada.net/traditional**
Greek houses apartments and hotels built
in the traditional architectural style, with
photos and links to each Website.

› **european-castle.com**
another good castle site; go to member castles then to castle hotels, good descriptions
and photos and links to individual Websites.

› **abitarelastoria.it**
Unterbringung an historischen Orten, in
Städten und auf dem Land, im Norden und
im Süden Italiens; Links zu allen angegebenen Orten, mit Fotos und Detailinformatio-
nen sowie Vorschlägen für Ausflüge.

› **agriturist.it**
Urlaub auf dem Bauernhof in der italieni-
schen Campagna; ländliche Anwesen, gast-
freundlich restauriert; regionale Küche und
ein Einblick in das Leben auf dem Land.

› **bedandbreakfast.com**
unkonventionelle
Übernachtungsmöglichkeiten auf der ganzen
Welt, die besondere Erfahrungen bieten;
detailreiche Informationen, viele Fotos,
Links zu einzelnen Webseiten und Online-
Reservierungen.

› **boutiquelodging.com**
globales Netzwerk von unabhängigen Hotels
und Resortanlagen mit einer kompletten
Aufstellung sämtlicher Anlagen.

› **castlesontheweb.com**
Webseite für Geschichtsfanatiker, Royalisten
und Romantiker, die Schlösser auf der ganzen Welt anbietet und bewertet – von König
Artus' Schloss in Cornwall bis nach Jamaika.

› **concierge.com**
Online-Adresse des amerikanischen Reise-
magazins Condé Nast Traveller mit Artikeln
und Links zu den Hotel-Hitlisten.

› **culturaltravels.com:**
Webseite für den kulturbewussten Urlauber,
nach Themen wie Kochen oder Religion ein-
geteilt; mit detailreichen Artikeln und Links
zu Reiseanbietern für jedes Gebiet.

› **dolcevita.com**
Tipps und Information rund um das italieni-
sche Dolce Vita mit Empfehlungen für
Wellness-Anlagen, Klöster und Bauern-
häuser; keine direkten Links, aber viele
nützliche Informationen und Kontaktangaben.

› **ellada.net/traditional**
griechische Häuser, Apartments und Hotels
im traditionellen Stil; mit Fotos und Links zu
allen Webseiten.

› **european-castle.com**
eine weitere Seite zum Thema Schlösser;
über member castles gelangt man zu castle
hotels; gute Beschreibungen mit Fotos
sowie Links zu individuellen Webseiten.

› **abitarelastoria.it**
hébergement dans des demeures historiques
en ville ou à la campagne, au nord et au sud
de l'Italie. Liens vers chaque établissement,
avec photos, informations détaillées et
propositions d'itinéraire.

› **agriturist.it**
séjours à la ferme au cœur de la campagne
italienne, dans d'hospitalières maisons
restaurées servant des plats régionaux
et offrant un aperçu de la vie rurale.

› **bedandbreakfast.com**
pour se loger hors de l'hôtellerie classique.
Une expérience originale à préparer grâce
à des informations détaillées, de nombreuses
photographies et des liens vers d'autres
sites, avec possibilité de réservation en ligne.

› **boutiquelodging.com**
réseau international d'hôtels privés, avec
toute une liste d'établissements.

› **castlesontheweb.com**
site pour amateurs d'histoire, royalistes
et grands enfants. Hébergement en château
dans le monde entier, depuis le fort du roi
Arthur en Cornouailles jusqu'à un château
en Jamaïque. Critiques indiquées.

› **concierge.com**
le site de Condé Nast Traveller, le magazine
de voyages américain. Articles de fond et
liens vers des « hot lists » d'hôtels.

› **culturaltravels.com**
site de vacances à thème, telle la gastronomie ou la religion. Articles développés et
liens vers des agences de voyage spéciali-
sées dans les vacances à thème.

› **dolcevita.com**
bons tuyaux sur la vie à l'italienne, avec
recommandations sur des stations thermales, des monastères et les séjours à
la ferme. Pas de liens directs, mais des
informations utiles recensant divers
contacts.

› **ellada.net/traditional**
maisons, appartements et hôtels grecs
construits dans le style traditionnel, avec
photos et liens vers chaque site.

› **european-castle.com**
un autre site de qualité sur les châteaux,
allant des châteaux-membres aux châteaux-
hôtels. Bonnes descriptions et photos, liens
vers d'autres sites.

Taschen Web Picks: click here for even more
places to escape to: Of course there are thousands of travel sites to virtual-visit on the
Internet, these are some of our favourites – but

› **fodors.com**
supplements the Fodor's Gold Guide book series with special features, advice from travel experts, discussion areas, and links. Great detailed list of hotels, no photos, but good descriptions and contact details, and gives picks for each place.

› **frommers.com**
Arthur Frommer's budget travel books on-line, very good information about many destinations, and detailed recommendations for places to stay.

› **gast-im-schloss-hotel.com**
a few of the best German castle hotels to stay at, links to individual Websites for photos and details.

› **gonomad.com**
for unconventional travel ideas, interesting unusual and off-the-beaten-path destinations with a wide range of outdoor cultural and alternative activities. Articles and top picks worldwide for places to stay, from eco-lodges to retreats.

› **hotelgenie.com**
efficient site with short list of hotels around the world, with helpful comments, links to Websites and direct booking.

› **lhw.com**
the Website for a collection of luxury hotels, "leading hotels of the world" both large and small, with photos, detailed profiles of each and on-line booking.

› **logis-de-france.fr & logis.it**
a series of small family-run hotels in Italy and France, ideal for holidays and stop-overs, even on a business trip; with descriptions, photos and links to individual Websites.

› **luxurytravel.com**
2,000 of the world's best hotels and resorts, selected from the best international hotel groups, privately owned properties and highly acclaimed label collections.

› **manorhouses.com**
hotels, manor houses, villas and cottages in Portugal.

› **marketingahead.com**
castles in Spain, palaces in Portugal, and luxury train travel; interesting sample itineraries.

› **fodors.com**
Ergänzung der Buchreihe Gold Guide von Fodor's mit Links, Ratschlägen von Reiseprofis, Diskussionsforen; detaillierte Hotelliste ohne Fotos, aber mit guten Beschreibungen sowie Kontaktinformationen und heimlichen Favoriten.

› **frommers.com**
die Reisebücher des gleichnamigen Verlags als Online-Version mit umfassenden Informationen zu vielen Zielorten und Empfehlungen für Übernachtungsmöglichkeiten.

› **gast-im-schloss-hotel.com**
einige der schönsten Schlosshotels Deutschlands mit Links zu den Webseiten der einzelnen Schlösser mit Fotos und Informationen.

› **gonomad.com**
Seite für unkonventionelle Reiseideen und interessante Ziele abseits der ausgetretenen Touristenpfade mit einem großen Angebot von Aktivitäten in Natur und Kultur; Artikel und Tipps zu Urlaubsorten auf der ganzen Welt – von Öko-Lodges bis Wellness-Anlagen.

› **hotelgenie.com**
effiziente Webseite mit kurzer, weltweiter Hotelliste, hilfreichen Kommentaren und Links zu Webseiten und zum Direktbuchen.

› **lhw.com**
die Webseite für Luxushotels, die »leading hotels of the world« – groß oder klein, mit Fotos und detailreichen Beschreibungen und der Möglichkeit der Online-Buchung.

› **logis-de-france.fr & logis.it**
kleine Familienhotels in Frankreich und Italien, ideal für Urlaub, Kurzaufenthalte und Geschäftsreisen; mit Beschreibungen, Fotos und Links zu individuellen Webseiten.

› **luxurytravel.com**
2000 der besten Hotels und Resortanlagen der Welt, ausgewählt aus den besten Hotelgruppen, Privathäusern und berühmten Label-Kollektionen der Welt.

› **manorhouses.com:**
Hotels, Herrenhäuser, Villen und rustikale Anwesen in Portugal.

› **marketingahead.com**
Schlösser in Spanien, Paläste in Portugal und luxuriöse Bahnreisen; interessante, ausgewählte Reiserouten.

› **fodors.com**
complète les guides Fodor's Gold Guide avec des rubriques spéciales, des conseils de voyageurs, des forums de discussion et des liens. Excellente liste détaillée d'hôtels, pas de photos mais de bons descriptifs et contacts. Vaste choix pour chaque destination.

› **frommers.com**
les guides de voyage en ligne de Frommers donnent de très bonnes informations sur diverses destinations, ainsi que des recommandations sur les lieux d'hébergement.

› **gast-im-schloss-hotel.com**
quelques-uns des meilleurs châteaux-hôtels d'Allemagne, avec liens vers des sites proposant des photos et descriptions détaillées.

› **gonomad.com**
site dédié aux voyages originaux et aux destinations insolites, avec toutes sortes d'activités sportives, culturelles et alternatives. Articles et sélection haut de gamme d'hébergement dans le monde entier, des bungalows écologiques aux retraites de luxe.

› **hotelgenie.com**
site proposant une courte liste d'hôtels dans le monde entier avec commentaires, liens vers d'autres sites et réservation en ligne.

› **lhw.com**
site spécialisé dans les hôtels haut de gamme, petits ou grands, avec photos, descriptions détaillées et réservation en ligne.

› **logis-de-france.fr & logis.it**
sélection de petits hôtels familiaux en Italie et en France, idéaux pour des vacances ou de simples haltes, voire pour des voyages d'affaires. Descriptions, photos et liens vers d'autres sites.

› **luxurytravel.com**
les 2000 meilleurs hôtels du monde, choisis parmi les grandes chaînes internationales, les demeures privées et les hôtels recommandés par les critiques.

› **manorhouses.com**
hôtels, manoirs, villas et demeures champêtres du Portugal.

› **marketingahead.com**
sélection de châteaux en Espagne, de palais au Portugal et de voyages en train de luxe. Bons exemples d'itinéraires.

be warned, you can spend hours roaming the Web finding great places to get away to; it's very addictive. Just add www. to these addresses, and bon voyage!

› **nationaltrust.org.uk**
a collection of holiday cottages in England, Wales and Northern Ireland, interesting and often historic buildings in special locations.

› **paradores.com**
state-owned chain of hotels in Spain which feature restored castles, palaces, convents and monasteries, along with modern hotels in special locations.

› **pousadas.com**
Portugal's historic hotels; pousadas are part of a network of more than 40 establishments that include the rich cultural diversification and the best traditions of the regions where they are located.

› **resortsandlodges.com**
a diverse selection, with photos and descriptions and links.

› **resortsonline.com**
top resort hotels and information for the luxury traveller, grouped under activities such as skiing and riding, or types such as spas and castles.

› **responsibletravel.com**
"holidays that give the world a break"; a diversity of pre-screened trips and accommodation provided by leading tour operators, accommodation owners and grass roots community projects.

› **simply-travel.com**
photos and details of handpicked houses, villas and hotels in Europe.

› **slh.com**
photos and descriptions of some 280 small luxury hotels, set in superb locations around the world. Each has its own character and appeal, whether a city sanctuary, adventure playground or spa destination.

› **taschen.com**
check in here for the best books to take on your holiday; and information about more books coming soon on great escapes around the world. Next, places in Africa, then Asia, then America. After that, maybe Space.

› **nationaltrust.org.uk**
Cottages in England, Wales und Nordirland, interessante und oft historische Gebäude in außergewöhnlichen Lagen.

› **paradores.com**
spanische Hotelkette im Staatsbesitz; angeboten werden restaurierte Schlösser, Paläste und Klöster sowie moderne Hotels in außergewöhnlicher Lage.

› **pousadas.com**
historische Hotels in Portugal; mehr als 40 Unterkünfte, in denen man den großen kulturellen Reichtum und die besten Traditionen der Regionen, in denen sie liegen, erleben kann.

› **resortsandlodges.com**
eine große Auswahl an Hotels mit Fotos, Beschreibungen und Links.

› **resortsonline.com**
die besten Resort-Anlagen mit Informationen für Luxusreisende, unterteilt nach Aktivitäten wie Reiten und Skifahren oder Art der Übernachtung wie Wellness- und Schlossanlagen.

› **responsibletravel.com**
»holidays that give the world a break« ist das Motto der Reisen und Unterkünfte dieser Webseite; sie werden angeboten von führenden Reiseveranstaltern, privaten Anbietern oder alternativen Interessengruppen.

› **simply-travel.com**
Fotos und Details von ausgesuchten Häusern, Villen und Hotels quer durch Europa.

› **slh.com**
Fotos und Beschreibungen von rund 280 kleinen Luxushotels an den schönsten Orten der Welt, jedes von ihnen mit besonderem Charme – ob nun als städtischer Zufluchtsort, Abenteuerspielplatz oder Wellness-Anlage.

› **taschen.com**
die besten Bücher für den Urlaub und natürlich auch Informationen über geplante Buchprojekte zum Thema Hotels der Welt in Afrika, Asien und Amerika und danach womöglich im Weltraum.

› **nationaltrust.org.uk**
choix de cottages en Angleterre, au Pays de Galles et en Irlande du Nord. Établissements intéressants, souvent historiques, bénéficiant de situations privilégiées.

› **paradores.com**
chaîne d'hôtels espagnols détenue par l'État, comprenant des châteaux restaurés, des palais, des monastères, ainsi que des hôtels modernes particulièrement bien situés.

› **pousadas.com**
site des hôtels historiques du Portugal. Les pousadas font partie d'un réseau de plus de 40 établissements reflétant la diversité culturelle et traditionnelle des différentes régions qu'ils occupent.

› **resortsandlodges.com**
sélection variée proposant des photos, des descriptions et des liens.

› **resortsonline.com**
hôtels de grand standing et informations destinées aux voyageurs aisés, regroupées sous diverses activités ou divers thèmes.

› **responsibletravel.com**
« des vacances qui respectent le monde ». Ce site propose un choix de voyages écotouristiques fourni par des agences de voyage de renom, des propriétaires d'hôtels et des projets communautaires locaux.

› **simply-travel.com**
photos et descriptifs de demeures, villas et hôtels européens triés sur le volet.

› **slh.com**
photos et descriptions de quelque 280 petits hôtels de luxe choisis dans le monde entier. Chacun a son caractère propre, qu'il s'agisse d'une retraite en pleine ville, d'un terrain d'aventure ou d'une station thermale.

› **taschen.com**
vous trouverez ici les meilleurs livres à emporter en vacances et des informations sur les ouvrages de voyage à paraître. Également, des sites en Afrique, en Asie et en Amérique. Prochaine destination : l'espace ?...

Taschen Web-Tipps:
Klicken Sie hier, um zu weiteren Traumdestinationen zu gelangen: Natürlich hält das Internet tausende virtueller Reiseziele bereit. Hier finden Sie einige unserer Favoriten. Doch seien Sie gewarnt: Man kann viele Stunden mit der Suche nach den schönsten Urlaubszielen verbringen – es macht süchtig! Setzen Sie den angegebenen Adressen einfach ein www. voran und dann bon voyage.

La sélection internet de Taschen :
Cliquez ici pour découvrir de nombreuses autres destinations : Parmi les milliers de sites de voyage qui existent à l'heure actuelle sur Internet, voici certains de nos préférés. Sachez toutefois que chercher une destination de vacances sur Internet est une activité fort absorbante ! Il suffit d'ajouter www. aux adresses suivantes pour plonger dans le monde du voyage virtuel ...

Photo Credits | Fotonachweis
Crédits photographiques

© 2015 TASCHEN GmbH
Hohenzollernring 53, D-50672 Köln
www.taschen.com

COMPILED AND EDITED BY:	Angelika Taschen, Berlin
ORIGINAL EDITION:	© 2002 TASCHEN GmbH
PROJECT MANAGER:	Stephanie Bischoff, Cologne
LITHOGRAPH MANAGER:	Thomas Grell, Cologne
TEXT EDITED:	Juliane Stollreiter/Delius Producing Berlin; First Edition Translations Ltd.,Cambridge
GERMAN TRANSLATION:	Claudia Egdorf, Düsseldorf; Gabriele-Sabine Gugetzer, Hamburg
FRENCH TRANSLATION:	Delphine Nègre-Bouvet, Paris
DESIGN:	Lambert und Lambert, Düsseldorf
PRINTED IN	China
ISBN	978-3-8365-5559-3

EACH AND EVERY TASCHEN BOOK PLANTS A SEED!
TASCHEN is a carbon neutral publisher. Each year, we offset our annual carbon emissions with carbon credits at the Instituto Terra, a reforestation program in Minas Gerais, Brazil, founded by Lélia and Sebastião Salgado. To find out more about this ecological partnership, please check: www.taschen.com/zerocarbon
Inspiration: unlimited. Carbon footprint: zero.

To stay informed about TASCHEN and our upcoming titles, please subscribe to our free magazine at www.taschen.com/magazine, download our magazine app for iPad, follow us on Twitter and Facebook, or e-mail your questions to contact@taschen.com.